Jacob Tik-Tok

Jacob Goes Back in Time with His State-of-the-art Prostheses

Robert Houben

This book is a work of fiction. Names, characters, businesses, organizations, places, events and incidents either are the product of the author's imagination or are used fictitiously. Any resemblance to actual persons, living or dead, events, or locales is entirely coincidental.

Printed in the United States of America.

For more information, contact :
houben.robert@gmail.com
https://www.roberthouben.com

Book design by Robert Houben
Cover design by Robert Houben

ISBN - Paperback: 978-1-7751575-6-4
- E-book : 978-1-7751575-3-3
First Edition: Agust 2023

CONTENTS

1 FALLING INTO TROUBLE

Jacob and Mark were playing on the floor of their father's office waiting room. It was a Friday afternoon and there was no one else there as the receptionist had called in sick that day. They had taken off their coats and packs and put them on the chairs behind them. They were laying on the floor between the chairs and a low coffee table. A magazine from the coffee table had become a car repair building where their cars would go for pretend repairs and "upgrades".

Jacob was 11 but still liked playing with cars. A lot of his friends were starting to think they were too old for that, but he had the excuse of playing with his 8-year-old brother Mark and it didn't really bother him if some of them thought they were too old for it. He was confident enough to stand out from the crowd. He had a feeling that there were more of his friends who still liked cars than would let on. When he visited them, many of them still had them scattered around their rooms.

Mark's car was driving across the rug toward their makeshift service station with Mark making a motor sound. Jacob had his car turn and drove it toward the service station, too. He was using his prosthetic hand to drive the car. Sometimes he was quite amazed at how natural it felt to move it.

Jacob had lost his right arm below the elbow and his right leg just below the knee in a car accident when he was just 2 years old. Before he was 3 he had started using artificial limbs. Artificial limbs were called prosthetics, which was a big word which he had mastered saying at a young age.

It was a professional day for the teachers, so their dad was taking care of them. He had work to do so they had come to the office and played in the waiting room until their grandparents came. They were going on a trip to their grandparents' place.

Jacob's prosthetics were both bionic, which meant it had motors. He had an uncle who worked for a laboratory where they did research and designed prosthetics, mostly for military veterans who had lost limbs, but also for other amputees. Often, they would have him try out prototypes for them, so he had the benefit of using new bionics before anyone else got to have them. He was aware of how lucky he was. He knew that his prosthetics were probably the best in the world. They had complex electronics, computer chips, batteries, and chargers, and were designed to react to the nerve endings and muscles on his stumps, making it feel like they worked just like his real hand and foot.

Jacob had enough spare batteries to play intensely for an entire long weekend. He also had the chargers for them with him, and lastly, he had a polymer blade leg that didn't need any power, just in case something went wrong with the electronics. They were prototypes and sometimes they malfunctioned.

Jacob's car was doing wheelies and crashed into the service station. The antics had Mark giggling.

Jacob grinned. He loved making his little brother giggle. Then something very strange happened.

Suddenly they were falling! Jacob fell about 2 feet onto a small bush. The coffee table landed beside him on the bush and began to roll towards him. He managed to push away from it with a shout and rolled off the bush but ran into the chair that had been behind him. It had dropped onto a bed of leaves and as he backed into it, his pack fell off of it and landed on him. The table was stuck on the bush, fortunately, and did not roll onto him.

Mark meanwhile missed the bush and landed on the soft ground on his stomach, knocking the wind out. His glasses flew off and landed on the ground a few inches from his face.

Jacob turned to Mark, frightened, and saw that Mark was already crying, trying to get his breath, and looking very frightened. Jacob started crying, too, from the shock more than anything else. The bush had scratched his good hand and his face a bit, but it didn't hurt enough to make him cry. It was the shock and fright that had him crying. For Mark it was both fright and having the wind knocked out of him.

"Where are we?" Mark asked when he got his breath back and had let up crying a bit. He picked up his glasses and put them on.

"I don't know!" Jacob answered. "I don't like this!" He stood up, glad to see that his prosthetics were working fine after the drop. With his good hand he checked that the prosthetic arm was still on firmly. The sleeve was well fitted, and the arm had not loosened from the fall.

The boys looked around. They were in a forest. The forest floor was a combination of mosses, leaves and needles from a few evergreens scattered through the forest, mixed with the deciduous trees. Down the hill there was a creek and he could see what looked like a well-worn trail running alongside the creek.

Anything that had been in the waiting room within about 5 feet of the coffee table seemed to be in the forest, in about the same relative position it had been in the waiting room. His toy car and Mark's car were in the bush. He reached in with his prosthetic hand to grab the cars and put his car in his pocket. He handed Mark's car to him.

The chairs that had been behind them with their coats were also laying on the ground.

"Grab your coat and your pack," Jacob said. "I want to check this trail down here."

The air was quite warm, and it looked like the sun was on its way down. That was odd, as it was only mid-afternoon. He looked at his watch to confirm. It was just after 3:00 pm.

Jacob picked his way around trees, balancing himself with his hands. The ground was not very good for walking on with an artificial. He wanted to be brave. He could hear Mark still sniffling and he hated to hear his little brother cry. He jumped down onto the trail from the bank above it. His prosthetic was good for that kind of thing. He turned around and helped Mark down. Then he gave him a hug. "We'll call dad. We'll get out of this OK," Jacob told Mark.

Mark gulped and tried to stop his tears. His brother's arms around him, even the prosthetic arm, felt very comforting. He had never actually known Jacob not to have prosthetic limbs, so they felt normal to him. "I'll be OK, now. I'll try to stop crying, but I was s-scared," Mark said.

"I know, I was too!" Jacob admitted, "I still am, but we need to look for help. We're not in Daddy's office and I don't think we're anywhere near it. Do you remember anything after playing with our cars on the rug?"

"No," Mark answered, still looking frightened, "you had just been silly and crashed your car into the service station, and then we were falling, and the office was nowhere."

"That's what I remember, too." Jacob looked at his watch. "It's the same time and day according to my watch." He pulled his pack off and reached in for his iPhone. He unlocked it. "The iPhone says it's the same time, too," Jacob frowned. That was very strange. He wasn't sure exactly what time they got to the office, but whatever had happened in between playing on the floor and falling into the forest had occurred in a lot less than an hour.

It was like something from a science fiction movie, or a bad nightmare! He wanted to wake up, but it felt too real.

He was trying to call his dad but realized that there was no signal. "We don't have a signal, Mark, we'll have to walk until we get one," Jacob told his little brother. "It might have broken from the fall. We may have to find someone to call Dad."

He looked around. Should they go up the creek or down? Down would be more likely to get to another creek and eventually to civilization. In this forest, up might wind up at a hilltop or a mountain. He looked toward where the creek seemed to go. "Mark, I think I see some smoke through the trees that way." He pointed down the trail. "That might be a house."

He reached for a bush. Taking it with both hands, his

prosthetic hand lower, he pulled the part of the branch above his prosthetic down with his other hand until it broke. Then he started scratching with his good heel in the dirt.

"What are you doing?" Mark asked.

"I've marked where we came out, in case we need to find it again, and I'm putting an arrow to show which way we went in case someone finds where we fell," Jacob answered. He had finished his rough arrow. "Let's start walking." Jacob reached out with his good hand and took Mark's hand in his.

Jacob noticed that the air felt quite a bit warmer than when they had first arrived at their father's office. There was a light overcast, but the ground was dry, and it didn't feel like it was going to rain. He liked the smell of the forest. Lots of leaves on the trees, and some wildflowers blooming. He told himself that he was having an adventure and would be brave for Mark's sake. That seemed to help him feel a bit better.

The boys walked for just a minute and the trail and creek both opened out into a field, the creek continuing across it. They could see a house through a row of trees on the other side of the field and the smoke he had seen appeared to be coming out of the top of the house. The trees blocked the view, but Jacob knew that it would be a chimney.

"That's where we'll go, Mark," Jacob said with a sigh of relief. "We'll call Daddy from there."

2 THE FARMHOUSE

The boys walked quickly across the field, following the trail that cut through it to the edge of the row of trees. They walk around the end of the row of trees and walked toward the front porch of the house.

As they walked toward it, Jacob noticed that there was no car, no wires going to the house, and the rough road that ran up to it beside the creek looked more like a trail than a road. There was a barn that might have a car, he couldn't see car tracks in the dirt, just what looked like bike or wagon tracks.

The house itself looked like something from an old-fashioned movie, except that it was in new condition and well kept up. It had a lovely, neat, flower garden with lots of blooms in it, with many different colours. There was a large stack of wood along the side of the house, all nicely cut up. He had been in an outback lodge with his father a few years ago and he was pretty sure who ever lived here used that wood to heat the house. There wasn't a single light fixture on the porch. Jacob had a worried feeling. Something felt wrong. He wouldn't let on to Mark, though. He paused and pulled his pack off.

"Whatcha doin' now, Jacob?" Mark asked.

Jacob was rummaging in the pack and pulled out some gloves. "I don't want to waste time talking about prosthetics when I knock on the door. I want to just get a phone, so I'm putting gloves on, so they won't be distracted by my prosthetics." He had them on, and the pack closed, and pulled it back on. With the gloves on, no one would know that his hand wasn't normal. "Don't mention my prosthetics. I won't unless they happen to bring it up. OK, Mark?" He had another reason for doing this. Sometimes when people noticed his hand or foot, they would treat him like he wasn't all there. They were likely to do that already because he was a little boy, but he really didn't want them doing this to him, now. He needed them to take their problem seriously. Somehow, he felt that it would just cause trouble. Besides, he hated it when people fussed over his prosthetics. He didn't mind explaining them normally, but right now it was a distraction he didn't want.

He took Mark's hand, and they walked up to the porch. Jacob was suddenly frightened, knocking on a stranger's door for help. His tummy felt like it was full of butterflies, but Mark needed him, so he took a deep breath and knocked on the door with his prosthetic hand.

There was a very un-adult sounding patter of feet running, and a young voice shouted "I'll get it!" Jacob took a deep breath, relieved. This place had children! That made him feel a bit better right away.

The door opened and a boy of about Jacob's height opened the door. Jacob on a quick guess figured that the boy was at least a year older than him.

"Hullo!" The boy said. There were two other children behind him. A girl about Mark's age and a toddler who looked about 3 or 4 years old. A man and woman came up behind them all. They were wearing clothes that belonged to the same old-fashioned movie that the house belonged in.

The family were staring at Jacob and Mark in a way that made Jacob uncomfortable. Jacob gulped, took a breath, and started talking. "Please, can you help us? We've gotten lost somehow, and we need to call our daddy on your telephone. Our cell phone isn't getting any signal." His voice broke partway through, and the tears started oozing out. It was with the greatest effort that he stopped himself from sobbing. So much for being in control! He was disgusted with himself but couldn't help it. He could hear Mark starting to sniffle beside him, too.

The family was looking at each other with funny expressions. The man shook his head. "Sorry, son, we don't have a telephone."

He had seen homeless children before and they never looked like these two. These strangers were cleaner than his own children, with clothes that looked immaculately clean, and that appeared to be made of material he'd never seen before with colours that made his head spin. He instantly concluded that they had to be children of a wealthy family. The smallest boy had glasses that looked like they would break if you breathed on them. He'd never seen a child that young with glasses, and that also convinced him they were from a wealthy family. A child that age had no real need for glasses, so a regular working-class family would never spend the money on them.

The woman had stepped forward, crouched, and pulled both boys to her. "You poor dears! We'll do what we can to help you."

"Is there a telephone nearby?" Jacob asked.

The man shook his head. "The nearest one's two towns away. We'd never get there before nightfall, now. It's too late in the day. How did you get lost?"

Jacob wiped his eyes. He was still trying to stop crying. This was not going very well. Now what would he do! If he told them about falling through the air from a waiting room, they'd think he was mad. He didn't want them thinking they were crazy. An idea came to him.

"Can you come with us quickly and we can show you something?" Jacob begged. "You won't believe me if you don't see it. You might if you do see it. It's only a few minutes from here, just past the end of the field on the other side of the trees."

The man looked hesitant. "When is supper ready, Mary?" he asked his wife.

"In about 20 minutes, but I can delay it a bit if I have to. You have time if it's close." Mary answered.

"All right," the man said. He pointed at his older son. "Jack, you can come with. The others stay here."

There was a short protest from the two younger children, but the man stood his ground. "Jack should be enough help," the man said.

The older boy and the man grabbed their coats, hats and boots and stepped out of the house, closing the door behind them.

The four of them began to step down off the porch.

"We might as well get your names," the man said.

"I'm Jacob Harper and this is my little brother Mark," Jacob answered.

"How old are you?" the man asked.

"I'm 11 and Mark is 8." Jacob answered.

"I'm Tom Rand," the man said, "and this is my 13-year-old son, Jack."

Jack had been frowning as they walked. He had good hearing and there was an odd sound coming from the older boy's right foot when he walked. Almost like there was water in his shoe, but not quite the same.

Jacob meanwhile noticed again that it was quite warm, especially with the gloves on. It was not that warm when they had arrived at his father's office. Somehow the day had warmed up a lot, very quickly.

When they got to the place where they had started, Jacob pointed at his arrow in the dirt. "This is the place. Here's the arrow that I dug in the dirt in case anyone came looking for us, so they'd know which way we went on the trail." Jacob took a step and pointed at the bush. "And I marked this place to show where we came down onto the trail. We really need to go into the bush there for a few feet." Jacob managed to pull himself up using his left hand on a small tree.

Tom and Jack looked at each other, noting how awkward Jacob looked clambering up the bank. Then they followed him. It was like he only wanted to use his left hand.

They followed Jacob as he led them a few feet to the place where the table and chairs were. Jacob had pulled out his iPhone and started videotaping the scene. It might come in handy later, so they wouldn't have to walk here again.

Jacob turned to the man who was staring at the table and chairs in puzzlement. "Here's what happened," Jacob started. "We were at our daddy's office waiting for him to do some work downstairs, and we were on the floor in the reception room, playing on the floor with our toys, and we had this table here, and these two chairs with our packs and coats on them here, and we were playing with this magazine here, and these books and these other magazines were on the table top, when all of a sudden we were falling onto the forest floor."

Tom and Jack were looking confused. Jacob sighed. "It doesn't make any sense, but neither Mark nor I remember anything happening in between those two things. According to my watch and the clock on my iPhone, it had to be less than an hour and probably more like a few minutes between us playing in the reception room and falling here. I fell on the bush right here, and Mark fell on the ground on his tummy right beside the bush here. It really scared us."

Tom had picked up the magazine and was flipping through the pages. He whistled. "This is amazing! Jack, look at the colour in this. And look at these pictures! They must be photographs, but someone has done a fantastic job of painting them."

He turned to Jacob, with a puzzled look. "So, as far as you remember, one minute you're playing in a room in a building and next moment you're falling in a forest with all the furniture and other things from that room falling with you, with no building in sight?"

"Yes, that's right!" Jacob answered. "Now you see why I had to show you this. You'd think I was crazy if you didn't see the furniture in the middle of the forest. Maybe you still think I'm crazy, but I'm not!" Jacob's voice broke. He was not sounding very in-control again. He was aware that he sounded like a frightened little boy. He struggled to gain control.

Tom was examining the furniture. "Look, Jack, this hasn't been out here for very long. I hate to leave it here, but it might be important for their folks to find these items." He turned to Jacob and Mark. "I'm going to take these magazines and books with me but leave the furniture here. Does that sound OK to you?"

"Yes," Jacob answered. "I think we should leave the table and chairs in case they come looking for us. I don't know how, but then I don't really know how I got here, anyways."

"OK, let's go have supper," Tom said. "You'll be our guests tonight. We'll see about getting you to a telephone tomorrow." He gave one last look at the furniture in the forest, a funny expression on his face.

Jacob stopped the video recording, and the iPhone made a sound as the recording stopped. The man gave him another funny look, but didn't say anything about the noise.

They walked back to the trail where they all jumped down the bank. Jacob jumped last, and as he jumped, his right pant leg rode up, and the stainless-steel shaft of his prosthetic showed for just a second.

"Daddy, there's something really odd about that boy's right leg!" Jack said.

Jacob sighed. He might as well get this part over with. He stopped, pulled up his right pants leg to just below his knee, showing the prosthesis, including where it attached to his leg. "I've got a prosthetic leg. It's bionic and has a motor that controls the ankle and compensates for me when I'm walking." He looked up at the man and boy.

Both had their mouths open in surprise. Tom found his voice first. "You're an amputee?" he asked.

"Yes," Jacob answered, matter-of-factly, "I lost my leg in an accident when I was 2 years old. I've been using prostheses since I was 2, but I just recently got this one. It's really amazing. If it didn't make a noise, you wouldn't know it was artificial." Jacob grinned.

Tom whistled. "That's really amazing! I've never seen anything like this before."

Jacob pulled his pants leg back down and straightened up. "It's probably the most technically advanced prosthesis in the world," Jacob told them, proudly.

Tom made a mental note that the boy used a lot of big words very comfortably. He was not only wealthy, but clearly very intelligent and educated.

As they walked along the trail, Jacob was conscious of both of them watching closely as he walked. Jacob was used to people doing this. Even those who were familiar with these types of prostheses were always fascinated by how well they worked. His uncle's staff would watch him closely with the prostheses for a completely different reason. They were looking for flaws and wins in their design so they could constantly improve it. So, Jacob was quite comfortable with the attention.

Jacob was also aware that having prostheses since he was a child had helped him to adapt. He'd met adults who had real trouble learning to use prostheses. He used them very naturally.

As they arrived back at the farmhouse, the younger children had been watching for them, so as soon as they started walking up the steps, the door opened.

"Mommy, Timmy, Alice!" Jack said excitedly, "You won't believe it, but this boy has an artificial leg with a motor in it! You can hear it whir really quietly when he walks!"

They were staring at Jacob and the man spoke up. "He had his leg amputated when he was 2 years old, so he has an artificial leg. You really can't tell, except for the sound it makes. Pretty impressive if you ask me."

"Can I see it?" The toddler asked.

Jacob grinned and pulled up his pants leg. The children's mouths dropped, but the mother gasped. "Oh, you poor dear! You come in at once and make yourself comfortable. Here, let me take your gloves off."

Jacob stepped back and grinned. "I kinda didn't tell you the whole story. The same accident took my right arm below the elbow, so that's a prosthetic too." He pulled the glove off and got another gasp from the family. His prosthetic hand was a grey metallic colour. He really liked it, because it looked really cool and space age, but there was no doubt when you pulled the glove off, you knew you were not looking at a human hand. He used it to pull off the other glove. The family all heard the soft whir of the motors in his right hand as he flexed it for them.

He pulled his pack and coat off and handed the coat to the mother who put it on a hook.

Mary took Mark's coat and put it up, too. She looked at Jacob.

"Normally we ask people to take their shoes off in the house, but I'm not sure if your shoe comes off that foot."

"It can come off, but it looks funny, like a doll's foot. It's intended to fit a shoe, not look real," Jacob answered. "My shoes were walking through damp fields and dirt roads, so I'll take them off."

He sat down and loosened the Velcro on both shoes, using both hands.

"How do you work that hand?" Jack asked.

Jacob smiled at Jack. He loved showing his knowledge of how his prostheses worked. "I move muscles on my arm right about here, and sensors in my sleeve detect that movement and drive the motors." That was the quickest and easiest explanation. There was a lot more, but that explanation usually worked for people.

Jack looked impressed. "That's really swell!"

Mark always loved it when people were impressed with his older brother's prostheses and what he could do with them. Despite being 3 years younger, Mark was very protective of his older brother. He would get into a very bad temper if anyone made fun of Jacob's disabilities or suggested that he was in any way inferior. Jacob was always trying to settle him down, yet he loved his little brother for it. The two were very close. Mark decided that he really liked Jack.

"Mark, can you help me?" Jacob asked. "It's really hard to get the shoe off, even with it untied. It fits pretty snug," Jacob explained to the family.

Mark stepped up and helped pull the shoe off the end of the prosthesis. He was used to doing that for his big brother and loved to help.

Jacob stood up and hooked the heel of the other shoe under the fake big toe of this prosthesis, pulling it off easily. "That one's a bit easier." He laughed.

3 SUPPER AND SOLVING THE MYSTERY

Well supper is almost ready, so everyone should wash up," Mary said. "I could have held it off a bit longer but it's ready now."

Jacob looked at his watch, puzzled. "Isn't it only about 3:30 in the afternoon? Isn't it kind of early for supper?"

Tom laughed. "Your watch is off. You may have had more than an hour to get where you were. It's 5:30. See the grandfather clock in the hall? We'll sort this out for you after we've eaten. Now go wash up and we'll eat first, then figure out what's going on."

Jack took a basin outside and filled it with water at a hand-run pump, and brought it in. The children all washed their hands in it. There didn't seem to be a tap in the house.

They went to the kitchen and sat at the table, and then everyone bowed their heads. This was familiar to Jacob and Mark.

Tom prayed. "Thank you, Lord, for this food that you have provided for us, and thank you for our two visitors who came to us today. Guide us as we seek to provide them with the help that they need, and give us wisdom to get them to their family quickly. In Jesus name, Amen."

Mark sighed. "I feel a bit better after that prayer," he smiled at the man. "But I still want my daddy."

Jacob and Mark enjoyed the food but weren't very hungry. They felt like several hours were missing.

While they ate, Jack described their walk and what they had seen to the family. Everyone was puzzled by how the table and chairs got where they were. Again, Jack made the comment about painting the photographs in the magazines. This puzzled Jacob, but he didn't say anything right away.

Tom insisted that they eat first and look at the magazines and books later. As they ate, Jacob had to explain more about his prostheses. He noticed that some things confused them, as if they had no idea what they were talking about. He had also noticed that there didn't seem to be a single electric light in the house. There were lanterns hooked up in various places on the walls.

"Do you have electricity, Mr. Rand?" Jacob asked.

"No, sorry son, we don't," Tom answered.

Jacob looked worried. He took another bite.

"What's the problem with that?" Tom asked.

"Well, my motors all run on electricity, so if I spend a couple of days away from a good source, my motors will all stop working. My leg will still work a bit, but it will be heavy and awkward, and my arm will stop moving," Jacob answered, "so I get nervous if I only have my electrics and I'm nowhere near a power source. I have my spring-loaded polymer leg in the pack. I don't like to play anything rough with the electrics, cause they're expensive. Usually if I go camping, I just take my cable hook hand and my regular spring-loaded leg. Then I don't care if don't have power. Also, the electrics get into trouble with water. They're electric so I have to protect them from too much water. I don't have a cable hook hand with me."

They had finished eating and Jack and Alice were given the job of clearing off the table. As they were clearing the table, Tom said "Too bad we didn't have a map of where your father's office was."

"It might be on your iPhone on the maps app?" Mark said to Jacob.

Jacob gave Mark a big smile. "Sometimes, little bro, you are a genius. I have offline Google maps of our area."

He got up and trotted down the hall, grabbed his pack and came back to the table. He pulled out his iPhone and unlocked it. He held it up to Mr. Rand and pointed at the clock on it. "See, the iPhone agrees with my watch, it's only 4:00, not 6:00. Weird, that they'd both be off!"

Tom stared hard at the device held in front of him. It looked like a piece of paper under glass.

Jacob pulled it back and began to poke on the glass. The entire family leaned over to stare as things moved on the glass! Their mouths were hanging open. Jacob saw this and looked worried. "Haven't any of you seen an iPhone before?" Jacob asked.

"I have never in my born days, seen or heard of anything like this," Tom answered.

Jacob got the maps app up. He was able to expand it to show his father's office. He held it out to Mr. Rand. "Here is where we live, this is our town, you can see the name here, and here is where my father's office is." He slid the display to show different areas.

Tom whistled. "Can I make it move like that? It's not magic, is it?"

Jacob frowned. "Of course, it's not magic. There's no such thing," he said disdainfully. "Yes, just put your finger down and slide it around. Don't tap and don't double tap and you'll be fine. If you use two fingers, you can expand or contract the map like this, to make it bigger or smaller, or rotate it."

Tom moved the map around shaking his head and saying "Amazing!" over and over again. Finally, he looked up at Jacob. "I believe I recognize things on the map, but there are no streets where most of the streets on your map are. I recognize this hill by its name. This area is named after our neighbor's farm, which would be about there. This here looks like the creek that runs past our house and here's where another creek runs into it just below our house, so we would be here." He pointed at the areas on the map as he spoke. Then he slid it over a bit. "Up here is where you say your father's office is, but it's just forest. In fact, your father's office would be right about where the table and chairs are." He frowned in thought. Something seemed quite odd about all this.

Jacob had that same feeling that he was in a science fiction movie or a bad dream. In the back of his mind, what Mr. Rand said seemed to be very important, but he couldn't make sense of it yet.

Tom decided to try a different approach. "What does your father do for a living?" He asked.

"He's a physicist." Jacob answered. "He's a research scientist who specializes in relativity theory."

"What's that, exactly?" Tom asked.

"Well," Jacob paused to think, it was probably very important that he explain it well, and he had learned a long time ago that the smarter he sounded the more likely adults would listen to him and take him seriously, "he studies space, time, energy, and matter and how they work together. He does some work for the government so he can't really tell us all that he does."

"I get the space, energy and matter part, but what can you do with time?" Tom asked. "Isn't it pretty straightforward?"

Jacob had run into people before who had a very simplistic view of time. His father had seen to it that he had a more rounded understanding, even if he was only 11 years old. "Time, space, and matter are all related. While you normally can only go forward in time, under the right circumstances you can actually go backward," Jacob answered, frowning, "but normally you need a ton of energy and a huge mass source like a black hole. My daddy studies how all these things are related."

The nagging feeling was growing that there were gaps in what these people knew and that it was all tied together somehow, and Jacob was frowning hard, trying to figure out how all this made any sense. It was almost like they really belonged in the same old-fashioned movie as their clothes and the house.

Tom reached to a counter behind him and grabbed the magazines and books that he had taken from the forest and put them on the table. There were gasps from the family, and for several minutes they were exclaiming over the pictures.

Jacob thought that was odd. Why were they so amazed with ordinary magazines?

"See how they've painted the pictures so realistically?" Mr.

Rand was showing a photo of some people to his wife.

"What do you mean by that?" Jacob asked. "Those are regular colour photographs."

"Photographs aren't colour, they're black and white, unless you paint them." Tom protested.

"Yeah!" Jack agreed.

Mark grabbed the iPhone, shifted it to camera mode, found the video that Jacob had recorded in the forest and started playing it. He held it out to them. "You mean you don't believe in colour pictures?" he asked. "Is this full colour?"

"Y-yes, it is!" Jack said stunned as the video ended. The other children and the adults had their mouths hanging open.

A thought had struck Jacob while Mark was doing this. "Are you Amish?" he asked Mr. Rand. He knew that Amish people would have nothing to do with new technology. It was part of their religion. Maybe these people were Amish.

Tom closed his mouth, looked puzzled and asked, "What's Amish?"

Jacob sighed. "You aren't. If you were, you'd know what it was. It would have maybe explained things. This is really weird."

"You made this movie of us, when you were showing us the furniture," Tom said.

"Yes," Jacob responded "I thought that way I wouldn't have to take someone back there again. I could show them, and you could confirm what they were seeing. You're in the video."

"Video?" Tom asked.

Jacob Looked puzzled. "Yeah, that's what you call a digital movie."

"Digital?" Tom asked, with a puzzled frown.

Jacob sighed. "It means that it doesn't need tape. It's all electronic."

Tom turned to the magazine and flipped a few more pages.

"What is this picture?" he asked, pointing at a picture of a plane in the sky, advertising a vacation company.

"That's an airplane." Jacob said.

"You mean a flying machine? I've never seen a plane like that before." Tom said. "Where does the pilot sit?"

"Right up here in the cockpit." Jacob pointed to the front of the plane.

"How big is it?" Jack asked.

"I don't know," Jacob shrugged, "I've been on a big one. I know there was a couple hundred people on it."

It felt pretty awkward in the room. The family was staring at Jacob like he had two heads and he was trying to figure out why they didn't understand anything. He almost asked them again if they were Amish, but even Amish people would know what an airplane was. They just wouldn't fly on one.

Mary was looking puzzled at one of the magazines. "What is this?" she asked, pointing at the outside cover.

Jacob looked at what she was pointing at. "That's the date of the magazine," He answered, giving her a puzzled look.

"I get the September part," she said, "but what's this number after it?"

Jacob gave them a look like they had two heads. "That's the year! Duh! Twenty twenty three!"

The entire family was looking at him again like he had two heads. Tom, with a funny look on his face asked, "What is today's date, in full, please?"

Jacob was staring at him. He took the iPhone from Mark, hit the home button, and went to the calendar app. "Here, this is the date the iPhone, my watch, Mark and I all think it is. It's Friday, February 23rd, twenty twenty three." He showed them his watch. "My watch says the same date, but it doesn't have the year, see?"

Mary said, "Well that's absolutely silly. That's an impossible date."

Jacob was starting to feel angry. "How can that be impossible?" he said in a frustrated voice.

"Well, it's only nineteen ten. This magazine won't have been printed for over a hundred years," Mary answered. "It's completely impossible."

Suddenly everything that had been nagging at him seemed to fall into place. "Oh!" he said and thought hard. 2023 – office, 1910

– only forest. His eyes got big and round, and his mouth dropped open. "Oh, No!" He groaned.

"What's wrong?" Tom asked.

"What is today's date? What do YOU think it is? In full?" He asked Mr. Rand.

"Today is Saturday March 19th, 1910." Was the answer.

Jacob looked stricken. The others watched him go red in the face.

"Oh no, oh no, OH NO!" It was all coming together. "Daddy! What have you done?" The tears were going down his face again.

"What is it, Jacob?" Mark looked frightened.

Jacob turned to Mr. Rand. "You have to tell me the truth! If this is a joke it isn't funny. Please tell me the truth, is it really 1910?"

"Yes, it is." Tom had a calculating look on his face.

"You promise this isn't a joke?"

"No, this is not a joke, that's really the date." The family were giving each other strange looks.

Mark was frowning. None of this made sense to him.

Jacob turned to Mark. "Daddy's lab is in the basement. It might be right under the waiting room. I think it is, actually. What if one of his experiments came up through the floor, and moved everything loose in our side of the waiting room through time to 1910? There wouldn't be a building. We had to take a few steps up to get to the first floor, so we would have been a few feet above ground level. We fell into a forest because that's what was there in 1910. Daddy has sent us back here by accident, and I don't know if he even knows where we are or what happened."

Mark's lower lip was trembling, the tears were streaking down his face. "Will Daddy be able to find us? Will we ever get home?"

"I don't know." Jacob answered. He gave up trying not to cry. It wasn't working anyways. He wasn't a crybaby, but this was a terrible situation, and he was very frightened!

Mary was trying to comfort Mark, who was crying hard. She looked at her husband. "Tom, do you believe this nonsense?" she asked.

Tom scratched his head. "I don't know, Mary. This thing he has that he calls an 'eye phone', this sounds like something we'd have in the future. We sure don't have anything like it now. He has a full colour motion picture with sound in that little, tiny box, and it's of us at the site where he fell, with no big reel of tape. That's impossible to fake, and I have trouble believing that anyone today can do that in something so small. It's like magic! And his artificial limbs with their motors, they're beyond anything I've ever heard of. And I've seen the table and chairs in the forest, you have too, for that matter. That thing of his showed it to you. That's exactly what we saw. I don't know how anyone could fake that, or these magazines and books, and even this children's book has a copyright and printing date in it that match what they're saying. What he just said makes more sense than anything I can come up with."

Jacob looked at Mr. Rand. "This is a bad thing. Who's going to care for us while we're waiting to see if Daddy comes for us? My prosthetics will run out without electricity. I'll outgrow them and need new ones. And I don't know if Daddy can even come and get us."

Mr. Rand was scratching his head. "Mary, I believe I need the advice of my friend Dr. Anton. We'll see him at church tomorrow. Maybe he can help us with the mystery." He turned to Jacob. "First thing, before we try to explain the whole story to him, we'll have to show him the furniture in the woods, your eye phone thing, and your artificial limbs. He won't believe us if we don't start there. For tonight, you'll stay with us. And tomorrow, you'll go to church with us."

4 LEARNING ABOUT TIK-TOK

The adults started asking all kinds of questions about the magazines. Jacob and Mark answered as best they could. One of them had a car commercial, and they answered questions about the cars. They even pulled their toy cars out and showed them. At one point Mark showed Jack the model name and year on the back. It was a 2009 model, so Jack noted it was a car from 99 years in the future.

Mark let Timmy play with his car and showed him how he rolled it and made motor sounds. Timmy clearly loved playing with it.

Jack wanted to know all about them flying on an airplane.

"Where did you fly to?" asked Jack.

"We flew to Paris one time." Mark answered.

"Across the water?" Jack asked, amazed. "How long did that take?"

"I sleeped. Jacob, do you 'member how long it was?" He asked his brother.

"I think it was about three or three and a half hours. It was a big jumbo-jet," Jacob answered. "Oh, you wouldn't know what that was... I think it held about 300 people."

As it began to get dark, the family lit lanterns that ran on kerosene. Jacob and Mark were fascinated with them. "I've never stayed in a place with lantern light before!" Mark said with a look of amazement.

They finally went into the living room, where the children were allowed to play until their bedtime.

"What do you like to play in the future?" Jack asked Jacob.

Mark spoke up with an answer. "Sometimes we like to play robot because Jacob's prosthetics are like a robot. He's part robot already."

Jack looked puzzled. "What's a robot? I've never heard of it before."

"Do you have stories of mechanical men?" Jacob asked.

"Oh yes!" Alice answered, "Don't you remember Tik-Tok the Machine Man in Ozma of Oz? Remember Momma read it for us, and how he helped Dorothy?"

"Oh ya!" Timmy hopped up and down. "I loved Tik-Tok!"

Jacob laughed, and started doing robot moves and a robot voice. "Then I am Jacob Tik-Tok, and this is my trus-ty ass-is-tant Mark."

Everyone laughed at the way he moved. Then he pretended to get his left arm stuck, making creaking noises as he pretended to try to move it.

"Mark, help me." He said in a monotone voice. "I ap-pear to be stuck."

Mark stepped over, pretending to pour something on the arm. "Here's your oil, Tik-Tok."

This began a time of play where they took turns trying to sound and move like a machine man.

At one point, Jacob asked a few questions about Tik-Tok, and Alice pulled out the Ozma of Oz story book and asked Jack to read a few parts about Tik-Tok. He started with the part where Dorothy found him:

For, standing within the narrow chamber of rock, was the form of a man--or, at least, it seemed like a man, in the dim light. He was only about as tall as Dorothy herself, and his body was round as a ball and made out of burnished copper. Also his head and limbs were copper, and these were jointed or hinged to his body in a peculiar way, with metal caps over the joints, like the armor worn by knights in days of old. He stood perfectly still, and where the light struck upon his form it glittered as if made of pure gold.

Dorothy found two cards that described what he was and how to use him:

```
+------------------------------------------------------------------+
|                                                                  |
|                         SMITH & TINKER'S                         |
|             Patent Double-Action, Extra-Responsive,              |
|                 Thought-Creating, Perfect-Talking                |
|                          MECHANICAL MAN                          |
|           Fitted with our Special Clock-Work Attachment.         |
|           Thinks, Speaks, Acts, and Does Everything but Live.    |
|           Manufactured only at our Works at Evna, Land of Ev.    |
| All infringements will be promptly Prosecuted according to Law. |
|                                                                  |
+------------------------------------------------------------------+
```

"How queer!" said the yellow hen. "Do you think that is all true, my dear?" "I don't know," answered Dorothy, who had more to read. "Listen to this, Billina:"

```
+--------------------------------------------------+
|                                                  |
|              DIRECTIONS FOR USING:               |
| For THINKING:--Wind the Clock-work Man under his |
|       left arm, (marked No. 1.)                  |
| For SPEAKING:--Wind the Clock-work Man under his |
|       right arm, (marked No. 2.)                 |
| For WALKING and ACTION:--Wind Clock-work in the  |
|       middle of his back, (marked No. 3.)        |
| N. B.--This Mechanism is guaranteed to work      |
|       perfectly for a thousand years.            |
|                                                  |
+--------------------------------------------------+
```

Dorothy had already taken the clock key from the peg. "Which shall I wind up first?" she asked, looking again at the directions on the card.

"Number One, I should think," returned Billina. "That makes him think, doesn't it?"

"Yes," said Dorothy, and wound up Number One, under the left arm.

"He doesn't seem any different," remarked the hen, critically.

"Why, of course not; he is only thinking, now," said Dorothy. "I wonder what he is thinking about."

"I'll wind up his talk, and then perhaps he can tell us," said the girl.

So she wound up Number Two, and immediately the clock-work man said, without moving any part of his body except his lips: "Good morn-ing, lit-tle girl. Good morn-ing, Mrs. Hen."

The words sounded a little hoarse and creaky, and they were uttered all in the same tone, without any change of expression whatever; but both Dorothy and Billina understood them perfectly.

"Good morning, sir," they answered, politely.

"Thank you for res-cu-ing me," continued the machine, in the same monotonous voice, which seemed to be worked by a bellows inside of him, like the little toy lambs and cats the children squeeze so that they will make a noise.

After reading a bit more, Jack skipped forward to a part where the metal man ran down.

"Now Tik-Tok," said Dorothy, "the first thing to be done is to find a way for us to escape from these rocks. The Wheelers are down below, you know, and threaten to kill us."

"There is no rea-son to be a-fraid of the Wheel-ers," said Tik-Tok, the words coming more slowly than before.

"Why not?" she asked.

"Be-cause they are ag-g-g--gr-gr-r-r-" He gave a sort of gurgle and stopped short, waving his hands frantically until suddenly he became motionless, with one arm in the air and the other held stiffly before him with all the copper fingers of the hand spread out like a fan.

"Dear me!" said Dorothy, in a frightened tone. "What can the matter be?"

"He's run down, I suppose," said the hen, calmly. "You couldn't have wound him up very tight."

"I didn't know how much to wind him," replied the girl; "but I'll try to do better next time."

This got lots of giggles from all of the children.

"At least my iPhone and my prosthetics tell me when they are running low!" Jacob laughed. "I have time to switch batteries."

Finally, it was time for bed. A brief devotional was held in the living room. The family read from the bible, then the parents said a prayer and the children repeated after them. They included a prayer that Jacob and Mark's father would come for them. The family's children went upstairs, and a rug was put down for Jacob and Mark to lie on, and some blankets for them to use.

Mark helped Jacob get his leg off, then his arm. The three Rand children were fascinated to see Jacob's stumps and asked him all kinds of questions about them.

They were especially amazed at how easily Jacob could hop around on just one leg and do things with one and a half arms. He'd do what he called his "stumpy walk" where he'd step on his stump and lower himself, then step on his left leg and raise himself up. He kept bobbing up and down as he walked, and he talked in a silly voice, pretending to get dizzy from all the up and down. This got giggles and laughs from the children.

Finally, the parents told their children to go upstairs to bed, and Jacob and Mark curled up on a rug with a blanket over them in the front room.

Jacob lay for a long time, unable to sleep. He kept thinking about what would happen to him if Daddy didn't find them. The more he thought about it, the bleaker the prospects seemed. There was a lump in his throat, and tears were running down his face. He noticed a sound from the kitchen. Mrs. Rand was coming in. She heard him crying softly and came over to him.

"Why are you crying, Jacob?" she asked, in a low voice.

"I'm scared! I don't know what will happen to us!" he answered. "We're like orphans, and in olden days people didn't take care of orphans very well."

She sat on the rug beside him and lifted him onto her lap, wrapping her arms around him. "We're not savages," she said, "You'll be cared for! And I'm sure if your father was able to send you here, he'll be able to come and get you!"

She held him for a few minutes until he stopped crying then laid him down, gently laying her hand on his head. Her hand was very comforting. In a few minutes, Jacob was asleep.

...

Mike O'Toole hummed as he stumped about his bakery with his wooden peg leg. He had lost the leg as a young man fighting in the Phillipine-American war. After being discharged he took over his father's bakery.

He heard the door open and turned to see Paul Rankin coming in. Paul was a relative newcomer to the town, but had worked for the great inventor Mr. Alexander Graham Bell, and wanted to become an inventor, himself. He was always trying to think of something that he could patent. He had tried a few things, and was able to sell a few of them, but had not had any big successes.

He and Mike got along well, and Paul would often come over to chat.

"Any new ideas, Paul?" Mike asked.

"I'm stewing on a few." Paul answered. "Nothing that I can settle on, yet though."

"I had an idea." Mike said.

"Oh?" Paul looked interested.

"Come up with a way for me to walk like I'm normal. Then

convince the government to pay for it for veterans and get yourself a nice government contract." Mike said. He looked down at his wooden leg. "This peg is better than nothing, but only just better."

Paul frowned. "That's not a bad idea. Let me think about it. I'll see what I can come up with."

The men chatted a bit longer, then Paul left.

5 TIK-TOK IN THE MORNING

Jacob woke up to the sound of people moving quietly in the kitchen. It took a second for him to realize where he was. He sat up, pulling his prosthetic arm over. He worked it onto his stump and turned it on, then used it to help get his leg on. He got up and walked to the kitchen. The adults were busy getting a fire going and preparing food to be cooked.

"Can I help?" Jacob asked. He loved to cook and felt the need to be helpful. It had come to him that he and Mark were at the complete mercy of these strangers.

Mary gave him a smile. "Of course, you can," she answered. "Do you know how to work a pump?"

"I saw Jack doing it, so it looks like a regular pump. I think I can handle it," Jacob answered.

"Then take this pot to the pump and fill it with water and bring it back here. Fill it to about here," Mary pointed just about an inch below the top.

Jacob took the pot and headed for the door. He put his shoes on and grabbed his jacket, picked up the pot and headed out the door. The pump was easy to work, and in a minute, he had the pot filled. He put the lid on and headed back to the house. He realized that it was quite warm, and he didn't need the coat. Given it was later in the year than what he had left behind at his father's office, that wasn't that surprising.

Inside he managed to work the shoe off his prosthetic leg

without help as he had not put it on tight.

Mark was getting dressed as he walked by with the pot.

"Here you go," Jacob smiled as he lifted the heavy pot onto the stove.

"Say, how'd you like to wake up my little sleepy heads for me?" Mary asked.

"I'd love to!" Jacob answered with a grin and headed to the stairs. Mark, fully dressed, followed him.

At the top of the stairs the door was open, and the Rand children were all sleeping.

Jacob put on his best robot voice and started moving like a robot. "Wake up! Wake up! This is the Tik-Tok a-larm clock service!"

Jack groaned, rolled over, saw Jacob moving and started to giggle. Alice and Timmy were also awake in a second and giggling.

Jacob continued in his monotone voice, noticing that Mark had come up behind him. "Rise and shine. The ear-ly bird gets the, gets the, gets the, gets the..." Mark gave him a slap on the back, and he finished "... gets the worm!" This was a game they often played together with other children to get laughs.

It got a torrent of giggles and laughs from the children who were now wide awake.

In a few minutes the children were all heading to a wash basin that their father had filled for them and washing up, playing Tik-Tok. Jacob and Mark washed up, too.

Then they went down for breakfast. The children were still in their nightclothes.

The adults had to put an end to playing Tik-Tok at the table as the children were all talking in monotones with gaps between their syllables, and they were giggling too much to eat.

When they were finished, the children went upstairs to put their work clothes on, then ran out to do their chores around the farm and then they came back and put their Sunday clothes on.

Tom came over to Jacob with a troubled look on his face. "Jacob, you had better not show off your hand or foot too much or draw too much attention to it. It might get people asking questions you don't want to answer for now."

Jacob frowned, thinking. "How am I supposed to do that?" he asked.

Tom answered "Well, when you walk, if you don't pull up your pants leg, no one will know about your leg. Remember, you fooled us. And you can put your gloves on, like you did for us. We had no idea."

"But someone's bound to figure it out. And they'll wonder why I'm wearing gloves inside when it's not even cold out."

"Well, maybe it won't work, but let's try." Tom said.

Jacob realized that Mr. Rand was genuinely concerned so he agreed.

Finally, everyone was ready to go. Tom brought the horse and wagon over from the barn, and Mark got all excited. "Oh! I've never ridden in a horse'n carriage before! This'll be fun!"

Tom looked at him with a funny expression. "How do you travel?"

Mark gave a ready answer. "Car, mostly, or bus. There are trains but we've never taken them, except in New York and in Paris. And sometimes we fly."

They chatted some more, and the children asked questions about how things worked in the future.

Then, up ahead Jacob could see a man walking, and immediately he noticed that the man had a peg for his right leg and walked with a cane. The man had red hair and a red beard and walked with a determined gait.

"Who's that man, with one leg?" He asked.

"Oh, that's Mike O'Toole, the baker," Tom answered. "He lost his leg in the Philippine-American war about 8 years ago. Came back and took over his father's bakery in town. He lives just over there, and you can see the church up ahead, so he walks, since it's close."

"Can I get out and walk with him?" Jacob asked. It was a rare opportunity to meet with a fellow amputee and when he did see one, he always felt that they understood him in a special way, and he understood them, too.

"He may not want you with him," Mr. Rand said. "He doesn't like people making a fuss about his leg."

"I'll ask him," Jacob said. Before Mr. Rand could stop him, Jacob called out. "Mr. O'Toole, can I walk with you?"

Mr. O'Toole stopped and turned. "Who are you, and how do you know my name?"

"I'm Jacob Harper, and I asked Mr. Rand here, who you are." He answered.

"And why would you do that?" Mr. O'Toole asked. "Do you feel sorry for me because of my leg?"

Jacob went red in the face. "No way! I hate it when people feel sorry for me!"

"Why would they feel sorry for you?" Mr. O'Toole asked.

Jacob pulled up his pants leg. "That's why."

Mr. O'Toole grinned and shook his head. "Well, I'll be. Yes, lad, come walk with me."

"I'm coming too!" Mark said.

The two boys hopped down. Jacob turned to the Rands. "I'll see you at the church in a few minutes."

Jack wanted to join them but to his dismay, Mr. Rand said no, and they were off.

"Shall I take your hand?" Mr. O'Toole asked, reaching his left hand for Jacob's right.

Jacob pulled the glove off and held it out. "I lost this at the same time."

Mr. O'Toole looked shocked for a second, then laughed. "Put the glove back on. You'll postpone the 'feeling sorry' for quite a bit and when they do find out, they just won't know what to do with themselves."

They all had a good laugh about that. Jacob put the glove back on and Mr. O'Toole took his prosthetic hand in his left hand, and they walked on.

As they walked, Mr. O'Toole asked about Jacob's prostheses. He was very interested in the different types that Jacob had, and Jacob showed him how the leg would help him walk, and how the arm would move based on the sensors picking up the muscle movement on his stump.

"Now that would be a very useful invention!" He said. "I suppose it's expensive?"

Jacob sighed. "It is, and I know I'm super lucky. They don't normally give these to children my age, but my uncle works with the engineers, doctors and scientists who do this, and I'm really good with them, so I get to test the latest inventions. We're always looking for ways to make them less expensive."

6 CHURCH IN THE WILDWOOD

They arrived at the church and Jack, Alice and Timmy all ran over.

Jack looked a bit put out. "I wanted to stay with you!" he complained.

Jacob went into his Tik-Tok mode. "I am sor-ry but I had im-por-tant bus-i-ness to do."

This got laughs from all the children nearby, and Mr. O'Toole laughed, too. The little boy clearly knew how to turn his handicap into a fun play with the other children.

The children all started laughing and walked robotically into the church. As soon as they got in, Jack said "OK, no doing that in here. We'll get in trouble. It's not respectful."

They sat down and soon a song service started. Everyone sang out of song books that had musical notation in them. Jacob had to show Mark how the verses worked. He knew because he had taken violin lessons with a special prosthetic hand for holding the bow. The first few songs were unfamiliar to them, but then they sang a song called "When the Roll is Called Up Yonder" that was familiar. A few songs later they ended with "Blessed Assurance" which they also recognized.

Then came the sermon. Jacob tried to follow it, but it soon got away from him and he started to look around at the people and the children around him. There were lots of children, and every family seemed to have 3 or 4 at least. One family had about 10 children, including a baby and a toddler. The oldest looked almost grown up.

Finally, a closing hymn was sung, followed by a long prayer and they were dismissed.

The children all filed out and down the street to the schoolhouse, where Jack told them they would have Sunday school while the parents visited in the church. Jacob went back into Tik-Tok mode and several children around them asked what they were doing. As soon as they heard, they joined in, although they didn't realize that Jacob was partly a real 'Tik-Tok'. Again, they stopped when they got into the schoolhouse.

Jacob and Mark took a seat close to Jack. A lady came to the front, and Jack leaned over to Jacob and Mark. "That's Miss Prentice," Jack whispered "she's the schoolteacher, but she's also the Sunday School teacher. She's really nice. You'll like her."

Miss Prentice led the children in a number of songs. There was one about "Dare to be a Daniel" that they hadn't heard before but really liked, and then they sang "Jesus Loves Me". Jacob's grandma and grandpa had taught them this song and he liked it and it was one of Mark's favorites, so they sang it with energy.

Next, they invited Jacob and Mark to the front since they were visitors. They sang them a welcome song, that embarrassed Jacob a bit, but Mark seemed to really like it. Then Miss Prentice said, "We have a surprise for our new visitors, so please hold your hands out and close your eyes."

The two boys did as they were told. Then Jacob heard Miss Prentice. "You should take these gloves off, dear, you won't need them in here."

Jacob opened his eyes and fought the urge to grin. "OK," he said. This would be interesting. "It might cause a bit of a scene," Jacob said.

"Don't be silly!" Miss Prentice said, frowning.

Jacob heard Jack saying loudly. "He's not, it will create a scene."

Miss Prentice frowned at Jack. "Jack, I'm surprised at you. Hold your peace."

"It's OK," Jacob said. "Your wish is my command."

He pulled the glove off of his right hand and tucked that one in his left pocket, while the whole room gasped, including the teacher. Then he used his prosthetic hand to remove the other glove. By this time the room had gotten extremely noisy. Somewhere in the room one child had said in a loud voice "He's really part Tik-Tok!"

Jacob shrugged at Miss Prentice. "I did warn you," he said. "It's artificial, a prosthetic hand. I lost my hand when I was a baby. Mr. Rand thought I should wear the glove to not make a scene. If it was up to me, I would have just let everyone make the scene up front and then get over it."

Miss Prentice had gone pale. Jacob looked worried. "Are you OK? Do you want to sit down?" He turned to a boy at the front. "Bring your chair here, quick and let her sit!"

The boy brought the chair over and they sat her down.

"Get her some water to drink!" Jacob said. "That'll help her."

One of the children ran over to a pail and brought a dipper of water. Miss Prentice drank it, and the colour gradually returned to her face.

"I'm sorry," Jacob said, feeling bad. "Some people react like that when they see it the first time. But please don't feel sorry for me." He grimaced. "I hate it when people feel sorry for me. I just want to be normal and have fun."

Miss Prentice tried to speak. "I… I've never seen a child with a missing hand before, it shocked me."

Jacob looked over to Jack. "Should I continue to hide the other part? I don't want to give her a second shock."

Jack looked doubtful. "I'm not sure she could take it just now. Hold off."

Jacob nodded. "Are you OK now, miss? I'm sorry I shocked you."

Miss Prentice nodded. "I'm OK now. Jack, I'm sorry I doubted you. You were right, it did create a scene." She laughed good naturedly. "I just never expected anything like that." She gave Jacob and Mark both a cookie, for being visitors, and sent them back to their seats.

They then broke up into groups based on age and separated boys and girls. Mark should have been with a younger group that was being led by an older girl, but he insisted on clinging to Jacob and looked like he would burst into tears when they tried to make him join the others his age, so they let him stay with Jacob's group of older boys.

The first thing Jacob's group did was an object lesson. Their teacher was the same one who led the singing and had nearly fainted. She had a needle and thread and asked for a volunteer to thread it from the older boys. Jacob had his hand up in a second.

"You can do it with your hand?" Miss Prentice asked, sounding surprised.

"You bet!" Jacob said. "This hand is super-steady, and I brace the other against it to do the needle."

He picked up the thread with his left hand and held it up so he could grab it with his prosthetic fingers. He licked it with his lips to get the end to cling together. Then he picked up the needle with his left, and balancing one finger against his prosthetic knuckles he threaded it expertly. "There!" Jacob said. "That wasn't so hard."

"OK", Miss Prentice said, "now pull that thread out and do it with this one."

Miss Prentice handed a short piece of rope to Jacob. Jacob laughed. "That'll never fit!" he said. "It's way too thick."

"No?" Miss Prentice asked, "What about this?" She handed him a wooden toy camel that was about 3 inches tall.

Jacob was giggling along with most of the boys. "That'll never fit either," Jacob said.

The lady took the needle from Jacob and let him sit down. Then she read a bible verse from the 10th chapter of the gospel of Mark about a rich young man who came to Jesus but left when Jesus demanded that he give up all his riches. The verses she focused on were 24-27:

"And the disciples were astonished at his words. But Jesus answereth again, and saith unto them, Children, how hard is it for them that trust in riches to enter into the kingdom of God!

It is easier for a camel to go through the eye of a needle, than for a rich man to enter into the kingdom of God. And they were astonished out of measure, saying among themselves, Who then can be saved? And Jesus looking upon them saith, With men it is impossible, but not with God: for with God all things are possible."

Miss Prentice explained that trying to be good enough to get into heaven was like trying to fit a full-sized camel through the needle. That the only way to get into heaven was by what Jesus did on the cross.

When the lessons were over, they all got to have a cookie and then were dismissed with prayer.

Jacob was impressed with her story, and when they had finished with their closing prayer, he caught her eye. "Miss Prentice, that was a really good story. I liked threading the needle, but you really made your point well. Thank you."

Miss Prentice pulled him to her and gave him a hug. "You're most welcome, dear. Now, you had something else you weren't going to show me and thought I couldn't handle it. Let me sit down and you can show me it. I should get it out of the way now."

In a second all the children had gathered around to see what Jacob would do. He reached down and pulled up his pants leg. "The same accident that took my hand also took my right foot, so this is my other prosthesis."

"Oh wow!" the children were impressed at this, and one said "He's really a Tik-Tok!"

Miss Prentice laughed. "I love that story, and yes, you've got a bit of Tik-Tok in you." She took this one a lot better but still looked a little pale. "I know you don't want me to feel sorry for you, but I can't entirely help myself. I just want to give you a hug and make it all better."

Jacob leaned forward and threw his arms around her. "Hugs I can do," he said. "And if you really have to feel sorry for me, just don't treat me different, OK?"

"OK!" Miss Prentice said laughing and looking better already. "I'll just love you like I do all my Sunday school children."

"Deal!" Jacob said with a shy smile. He could tell she really loved the children, and he really liked her for it.

As they left the building the children all gathered around him begging him to play Tik-Tok. Jacob shifted into Tik-Tok mode walking stiffly with his arms and legs moving strangely. "We should re-turn to your par-ents now. They will be wai-ting! All wind up and start walking!"

This got a peal of laughter from the children who instantly all started playing the game together. Jacob pressed his finger into Mark's belly button and twisted. "I am wind-ing you up." he said, as Mark squealed with laughter. This got the other children doing the same thing. After several minutes of shrieking and giggling, an army of little Tik-Toks walked across the lawn to the church where the adults were gathered.

Tom had cornered up Dr. Anton before the church service started and had told him just a few facts about Jacob and Mark but had also told him there was more he had to see to believe. The doctor had agreed to come for lunch and look into the mystery.

After the service, a number of adults had gathered to ask about the visitors and Tom explained that they had got separated from their father in the forest and came to their door for help. Everyone agreed that they were clearly from a wealthy family. Even the wealthiest family in their community didn't buy play clothes like that for their children. They were still talking as the children came walking stiffly over.

"For land's sake, what are those children playing at now?" a mother exclaimed!

Tom laughed. "They're playing Tik-Tok, the machine man! Jacob and Mark like to play that, and they get them all going. I had to stop it this morning or they would never have got through breakfast!"

Dr. Anton loved children, and instantly got into the game with them. With a twinkle in his eyes, he shouted. "Take cover! It's an army of metal men!"

This got laughs from the children and several walked stiffly up to him. He grabbed one little boy and picked him up. "Where is the key to unwind him?" he asked, pretending to feel for it and using it as an excuse to tickle the child. The child squealed with laughter. Two other children came up to him begging him to unwind them too. He tickled a few more, then told them to shoo, and attack someone else, with a pleased smile.

"Jacob! Mark! Come here." Tom called. He frowned. "You took the gloves off!"

"The teacher insisted," Jacob explained. "Then she almost fainted and I felt really bad. It would have been much better if I had just had them off in the first place. The shock was almost too much for her. But she got over it and I even showed her my leg afterwards, and she was OK then."

A number of parents gathered around and stared at his prosthetic hand, exclaiming about it.

Dr. Anton had taken Jacob's hand and was examining it. "You can make this move?" he asked.

"Yep!" Jacob answered and opened and closed the hand and wiggled all his prosthetic fingers.

Dr. Anton asked him how it worked, and he gave the same explanation that he had given Jack.

Dr. Anton whistled. "How does it power the motor?" he asked.

Jacob unzipped his coat and pulled his right arm out of the coat sleeve. He unbuttoned his shirt cuff and pulled it back. He popped open the battery compartment. "It's electric. This is the switch you use to turn it off. Then you can remove the battery and put another one in. I have spares with me and there are more, and a charging unit in my backpack at their house." He closed the compartment and pulled his sleeve down.

The parents and children had gathered around and were clearly awed by what they saw. They had some experience with electricity. A few homes in town had it, although telephones hadn't made it there yet. To many of them it was like magic, and most of them didn't grasp how far advanced what they were seeing was.

Most of the children were still gathered around him, and a girl spoke up. "He has a fake leg, too. You should see it."

Dr. Anton frowned. "You walk like you have a normal foot.

How do you do that?"

Jacob pulled his pants leg up. "This foot has sensors and motors in the ankle. It detects what I'm doing and adjusts its motors electronically, in real time, to help me. It helps me walk up and down stairs, run, jump, step backwards, all kinds of things. It's the closest to a real ankle. It's probably the most technically advanced prosthetic in the world."

Dr. Anton noted the big words that the boy used easily. Most adults in this town could not talk like that. He shook his head and turned to Tom. "OK, I'm sold, Tom! I'm coming over for lunch."

7 THE DOCTOR'S PROGNOSIS

Dr **Anton arranged** to take the children back to his house where he would take his bag and let his housemaid know where he was in case a patient needed him. That way Tom and Mary could run ahead and start the lunch.

On the ride, Dr. Anton had more questions for Jacob. "How do the sensors translate the motion of your muscles on your stump to instructions to a motor?"

Jacob knew how this worked and loved to show off his knowledge. "When my mind sends the signals through the nerves to the muscles in my stump, these nerve impulses make electro-magnetic signals. These are detected by little electro-magnetic receivers in the sleeve. They feed this to a computer chip that's programmed to drive the motors."

Dr. Anton stroked his beard with the hand that wasn't holding the reins. "I get the first part, but what is a computer chip?"

"Oh..." Jacob frowned. He looked at Jack. "You don't have computers yet, do you?"

Jack laughed. "I have no idea what you're talking about, so probably you're right."

Jacob turned back to Dr. Anton. "Imagine a machine that you could put words into it, to ask it a question, or to ask it to do a job with words or numbers, and you could give it instructions to do whatever you wanted it to do. Now imagine that you take the input from the sensors and turn them into numbers and tell that machine how you want it to convert those numbers from those sensors into instructions to the motors. That's what a computer is. It's also electrical."

Dr. Anton nodded. "You mostly lost me, but I think I know the concept. Babbage's inference engine, but in electrical form."

"Oh, yeah," Jacob said. "I remember one of daddy's friends talking about that, long ago, how he started the idea of computers. He got his money from a lady with a funny name."

"Lady Lovelace." Dr. Anton said.

"Yes! That's it!" Jacob said. "Now you get it."

Dr. Anton gave Jacob a funny look and shook his head. He wasn't entirely sure he got it, but he'd leave it for now. They rode for another minute, then he asked. "Why did you call it a computer CHIP?"

"In order to make it fit in my arm and not be really heavy, you have to miniaturize it," Jacob answered. "If you could open up my arm, you'd see that the sensors have wires that lead to a bunch of little black square chips, mostly the size of my thumbnail. The inference engines are in those." Since Dr. Anton didn't know what a computer was, he'd use the word that the man was familiar with. "They're so small you can't see the wires in them." Jacob frowned. "They aren't actually wires, they're chemicals etched into the chip to make them conduct. I don't know how they do the memory, but it stores all the instructions you give it, too, and it can hold a lot of instructions."

They had arrived at Dr. Anton's house, and he told them to wait there while he ran in and spoke to his housemaid. He grabbed some boots, as he had been told that he would take a few steps into the woods. Then he took his bag out to the wagon, climbed into it, and turned it around, beginning the ride to the Rand home.

"Tell me about where you live," Dr. Anton asked.

Jacob shook his head. "I don't think that's a good idea until you see what I showed Mr. Rand. You'll have to wait for that."

Dr. Anton looked surprised, but Jack spoke up. "He's right, that's why Daddy told you you'd have to come out and see it. It really is a puzzler, and you won't believe it until you see it yourself."

Dr. Anton shrugged. He could wait a bit to get his answers. He asked more questions about Jacob's electronic wonders, and Jacob explained what he could. Dr. Anton was amazed at what the boy was telling him. He didn't realize that the world of electrical inventions had progressed so far, so quickly.

When they arrived, Tom came out and met them. This time all the children were allowed to join the walk. They crossed the field and walked down the trail, quickly arriving at the markers that Jacob had made to show where everything had happened. They climbed the bank and walked over to where the furniture still was. Dr. Anton marveled at how well Jacob could walk even in the rough forest.

Dr. Anton looked at the furniture, puzzled. "How did this get here?" he asked.

Tom looked at Jacob. "Tell him what you told me, just as you told it to me. Leave out your more recent conclusions until we get back to the house."

Jacob grinned. He pulled out his iPhone and replayed the video clip from when he explained it to Mr. Rand. Dr. Anton's eyes nearly came out of his head. He stood there speechless when it was finished. Mr. Rand explained that he had taken the books and magazines and that the boys' packs were at the house. "We'll go back to the house, and you'll see some the books and magazines and more of that thing they call an eye phone."

They returned to the house and Tom brought Dr. Anton the magazines and children's books. The doctor was stunned by the magazines. "The colour is amazing." he said. "They look like photographs that somehow captured colour. I've seen painted pictures, but these are so realistic!"

"They are colour photographs," Jacob said.

Dr. Anton was looking at an ad for medication. "Is this for real?" he asked, amazed. "No one has a cure for this."

"Well," Jacob said, "we do."

Dr. Anton gave him a funny look.

Mary had come out of the kitchen and took the magazine from

Dr. Anton. She turned it over and showed him the date. "It claims to be from the future." She walked back into the kitchen.

Jacob had the iPhone out. "Here's the current date and time according to my iPhone, and my watch agrees with it."

Dr. Anton stared at it. "That's absurd!" he said, frowning.

Jacob switched to the maps app. "Here is Daddy's office where we were. The maps app shows the last place that it knew where we were."

Mr. Rand stepped in and took it. "I've actually figured out how to move this with my fingers. It's really easy to use, but it absolutely amazes me to use it. Here is the creek outside our house and the small river it runs into. The office with all the streets around it is located right about where the furniture was." He looked at Jacob, "Now explain what your father does for a living in twenty twenty three."

Jacob looked at Dr. Anton. The man had a look of complete disbelief and shock on his face. "Hear us out, please," he begged.

Dr. Anton got a calculating look on his face and looked down at the iPhone. "Go on," he said, still frowning.

"My father is a physicist." Jacob continued. "He studies time and space and the relationship between them. It's a field called Einsteinian physics, but I'm not even sure if Einstein has been born yet, so I don't think you'll have any idea what that is. It's the study of the relationship between them. He works for the government, so we don't know exactly what he's doing but one thing that you don't know yet, is that it's theoretically possible to go backward through time." Jacob knew that this was where he usually impressed adults. The problem here is that whereas most adults he had talked to previously knew that what he was saying was true, these adults would find it hard to believe. He continued. "Supposedly it's close to impossible because of the energy and mass required, but not completely impossible. Also, you think time is constant and it's not. When you get really fast trains, you'll find out that time seems to move different for things moving really fast as opposed to things going slow."

Dr. Anton stared at the 'eye phone' and muttered. "And back

in the forest I watched full colour motion picture with sound, no less, in something so small I could put it in a pocket!"

Jacob gave a little laugh. "You have no idea what all that iPhone can do. You've only scratched the surface of its capabilities. Its best stuff happens when it connects to the internet, but you don't have Wi-Fi, or cellular, or internet of any sort, so that's kinda useless. I can use it to program my leg, too. It does it over wireless called 'Bluetooth'."

He looked at Dr. Anton. "Do you need a minute to take this all in, or should I go ahead with what I think has happened?"

Dr. Anton looked at him. "You might as well finish me off!" he said with a wry laugh.

"I think my daddy was doing a time experiment in his lab, which was below our waiting room, and somehow it affected the things on our side of the waiting room. We were taken through time from twenty twenty three to nineteen ten. The office wasn't there anymore, and we were a few feet above the ground so we both fell, along with the furniture and books. Now we're waiting for our daddy to figure out what happened to us and to come back for us," a look of worry crossed his face, "if he can."

Both boys had gone pale at the thought. Dr. Anton looked at the two boys closely. That look of extreme anxiety fixed it for him. These children couldn't fake that. In fact, there was no way that anything he had seen could be faked. The prostheses were impossible with anything that he knew was available at this time. The "eye phone" device was simply astounding! These children had to be telling the truth!

Jacob had watched the expression on Dr. Anton's face go from shock and disbelief to dawning understanding. The relief was huge, and he found that tears of relief were stinging his eyes.

"Well, I'll be a donkey's rear end!" Dr. Anton said, stroking his beard. This got giggles from the Rand children, and relieved grins from both Jacob and Mark.

From the kitchen, Mary's voice could be heard. "Doctor! Mind the children and watch your tongue!"

"Sorry, Mary! I've just had a grand shock!" he said laughing.

Then in a serious voice. "Everything in me says this is impossible, but then, everything you've shown me is equally impossible." He looked at Jacob. "Your explanation actually works, so I'm going to have to go with it." He sat back on the couch and picked up another magazine. "Arthur Conan Doyle, the writer of a story called Sherlock Holmes quotes his character as saying, 'Once you eliminate the impossible, whatever remains, no matter how improbable, must be the truth.' I guess you've never heard of Sherlock Holmes, though."

Jacob grinned. "'Elementary, my dear Watson.' Yes, I have! That's one story that never gets old."

Dr. Anton asked about things he saw in the magazine. Cars and planes. He was amazed to hear about the children flying in a plane across the Atlantic to Paris in just a few hours. He started to ask them about medicine and was amazed to hear about cures for cancer, heart transplants, artificial hearts, and Jacob tried to explain genetics, but he didn't really understand it well. He was really good with prosthetics, but for other topics he ran out of information very quickly.

They were discussing what the doctors had had to do when Jacob had his accident, when Mary called them to lunch.

Lunch was a lovely hot meal of fried pork with potatoes and carrots and bread with fresh butter. The adults had wine and the children had milk that was richer and creamier than anything the two boys had ever tasted, as it came fresh and unpasteurized.

When they had finished, Dr. Anton sat back and looked at Tom. "I've been thinking. Jacob has explained how his electronic prostheses will run out of power in a day or so, so I'm going to suggest that he and his brother come and stay at my house. I have electricity. He can charge his batteries there. I'll send them to the school in the morning, so your children will get to see them there. I'd like to examine him using his prostheses and see if I can get any ideas that I can use from them. In return for that information, I'll feed them for now, until their father turns up, which I'm sure he will. What do you think, Tom?"

Tom nodded. "That makes sense. I'm comfortable with the

children – they're good children and fun, but I'm a fish out of water with their situation, and not sure how to deal with his artificial parts when they run out of battery power."

Dr. Anton looked at Jacob and Mark. "Is that OK with you two?"

Jacob nodded. "It felt good to be around other children, but I really want to keep my prostheses charged. And I think Mark just wants to stay with me. It'll be fun to go to school with Jack and Alice. I guess Timmy doesn't go to school."

Dr. Anton nodded. "Good. It's settled. I'll stay around for the afternoon unless I get called to see a patient. That'll give you more time to play with the children. And some of the children you were playing with at church are my neighbors, so you'll have no shortage of little playmates."

A soft double-beep came from Jacob's leg. "Oops! I have to change the battery. It's getting low." He jumped up and ran to his pack and pulled out the battery. He crouched and pulled up his pants leg. Dr. Anton had followed him, and Jacob recognized that this was part of the bargain, so he explained what he was doing as he turned off the leg and why it was important. He removed the old battery and put a new one in. Then he turned the leg back on, and it gave a soft tone to indicate that it was working. He explained the different tones that the leg would set off to notify you of problems or that it was starting up.

They sat on the floor together and Jacob explained to him how the leg would shift in different ways. He explained how different movements would help him go up or down stairs and demonstrated with his good foot. He also showed how he could program it in different ways with the iPhone. Dr. Anton was pleased. The boy understood what he wanted to know and was already helping him to understand. He was also amazed at how well the little boy could explain the physics of the highly complex prosthesis. But then, this was near and dear to the boy's best good, and Dr. Anton had learned that even younger boys, when it came to something that they were passionate about, could be more knowledgeable than many adults around them.

He let Jacob go and play with the children. And Jacob played Tik-Tok with them. The children had stopped calling him Jacob and most of the time he was "Tik-Tok" to them, even Jack getting lost in the game they were playing.

Mark and Timmy went off by themselves for a while. Mark borrowed Jacob's toy car and let Timmy use his. Mark liked being a "big brother" with the little toddler.

...

Mike O'Toole called out to Paul. "I've seen your next invention."

Paul smiled. "Oh? What is it?"

Mike shook his head. "Did you see those two new boys? The ones that were lost?"

Paul nodded. "Yes, I saw them."

"Well, you should check out the older boy's prosthetics. If you could do even a fraction of what they do, that government contract would be yours." Mike said.

"I'll have to do that." Paul said, looking interested. "Where are they staying?"

"They were with the Rands, but the Rands were getting Dr. Anton to check them out." Mike answered. "I'd check with the doctor tomorrow."

...

Andrew Harper stood staring at the empty waiting room, confused. Where were his children, and where was the furniture?

"Jacob! Mark! Where are you!?" he shouted, a dawning sense of worry gnawing at him.

His co-worker Rob walked into the room and stared at it.

Andrew was looking out the window, both up and down the street. No sign of anyone anywhere.

"Maybe they're in the washroom." He said, looking puzzled. Even if they were in the washroom, they wouldn't have taken their coats and packs with them. And where was the furniture?

"Oh no!" Rob said. He'd turned pale. "No! No! No!"

“What’s wrong?” Andrew asked, annoyed that Rob would try to change the subject. He needed to know where his children were.

“Don’t you see what’s happened?” Rob asked, a look of dawning horror on his face.

“No. Does it have to do with my boys?” Andrew asked.

Rob looked him in the eye. “The lab is right below us. Our experiment partially worked, but we got all that dirt coming into our room. You remember we saw something dropping on top of the dirt pile just as we were turning the machine off?”

Andrew understood what Rob was saying, now. “Oh Lord, what have we done?” he groaned. “I’ve sent my two boys back in time!”

The rest of the team had come into the room while they were talking and were staring at the empty room.

“We’ll have to go after them.” Meg said. “We’ll leave all the settings the same, so we go back to the right time. Come, everyone, we need to figure out how to undo what we’ve done. We need a plan!”

8 THE DOCTOR'S HOME

Finally it was time for Dr. Anton to leave with the two boys. His housemaid would be preparing a meal for them, and he had to notify her that she had two young guests to feed as well.

As Jacob climbed into Dr. Anton's cart with Mark beside him, he turned to the Rand children and in his Tik-Tok voice said "Do not fret my friends. I will see you to-mor-row at the schoolhouse." He turned his head robot-like, and the children all laughed.

"See you tomorrow, Tik-Tok!" The Rand children shouted as they rode down the track. Jacob raised his prosthetic hand in a last robotic wave.

Dr. Anton was smiling. "So, in twenty twenty three, do they have Tik-Toks?" he asked.

Mark spoke up. "Yes, but we call 'em Robots. I never heard of Tik-Tok till we came here."

"Yes, we have robots," Jacob said, "but they still have a long way to go. It's really hard to make something that can think like us. Even understanding spoken language is hard for computers. It's extremely hard, but they're getting better really fast. Something like Tik-Tok is a dream, but we have a way to go before we can do that. The story about the Wizard of Oz is popular, because they've done movies about it, but I never knew there were other stories about Oz. I really like Tik-Tok. The best robots we have are called NAO. That's a acronym N-A-O. I don't remember what it stands for, but I think the middle letter stands for Alderbaran. They're a company that makes some of the robotics that go into my prostheses, so I know them pretty well. Their robots are really cute and fun to play with."

Jacob explained more about technology and spent some time trying to explain how you programmed the robots to do different things.

Finally, they pulled into Dr. Anton's home. A servant came out and took the horse and carriage into the barn. Dr. Anton took the boys into the house and introduced them to the housemaid Jessica. He explained that Jacob had two prostheses and that this was a word for artificial limbs. They would be staying with him for the time, and they would be eating supper today.

Jacob and Mark both liked the lady. She was young and strong and very cheerful, and immediately took to Jacob without seeming to feel sorry for him.

Dr. Anton showed them the room with the bed that they would be sharing and had them put their packs down. Then he brought Jacob down to his office and showed him the power plug in the wall. "This is the latest Hubbell adaptor," he said with pride.

Jacob remembered how in France and London he had needed adapters for the plugs and was relieved to see that the plugs were the right shape and size. He hadn't thought about that. He didn't know what a Hubbel adaptor was. "What voltage is this?" he asked. "Is it AC or DC?"

Dr. Anton raised his eyebrows. Few adults in the town would know to ask this. "It's 110 volts AC, 25 hertz."

Jacob was reading the notes on his charger and nodded. "That should work. Let's try it." He plugged the charger in, and the green light came on. Then he plugged the first battery in and the light beside it went red to show it was charging. He loaded up the charger unit with the batteries that had already run down. He plugged his iPhone into the USB charger jack. It pinged to life, showing that it was charging.

Mark was looking out a window, grinning. "Jacob, there's some of the kids from the Sunday school outside. I think they wanna play."

The children called through the window "Please doctor, can Tik-Tok come out and play with us?"

Dr. Anton looked up and grinned. "I think, Mr. Tik-Tok, you should go out with your trusty companion Mark-Tok and play with them until supper is ready."

Jacob stood up and looked out, grinning. He recognized the boys and girls from the Sunday school and he and Mark ran outside to play while the children outside ran to the front of Dr. Anton's house. As Jacob stepped out the door, he and Mark shifted into robot mode.

"Let's find some-one to play with, Tik-tok," Mark said, in robot mode.

"Yes Mark-Tok," Jacob replied, "let us play with these children!"

They played and had fun with the children until supper was ready. Jessica called to them. They walked into the house stiffly, in robot mode, and waved at the other children. They stopped playing robots as soon as they were in the house.

"That was fun, Jacob," Mark said, with a happy grin.

"Yes, it was." Jacob sighed. It was funny how playing with other children could make you forget your troubles.

They washed up, pleased to find that this house had some indoor plumbing, and came to the table. As they ate, Dr. Anton asked them about what they played with the other children. Both Mark and Jacob gave him an excited account of the stories they played with the children. Pretending to defeat all kinds of deadly enemies with their robot arms and legs. The other children pretended to be metal men as well.

Dr. Anton and the housemaid both laughed at the children's excitement at recounting their stories. Jessica had been a bit unsure at Jacob's missing limbs at first and wasn't sure how to treat him. She wasn't sure if he'd feel sorry for himself and fuss but was relieved that he seemed to be just a normal little boy who liked to play with other children and didn't fuss about his handicaps. She really liked the two boys.

After supper, Dr. Anton took them into his study where he had them show all the apps that they had on the iPhone and explain them. They had only got through a few of the built-in ones before it was time to go to bed.

Dr. Anton asked to watch while Jacob took his prostheses off. He examined Jacob's stumps and was very impressed with the professional job that had been done by the future doctors.

As they crawled under the covers, Dr. Anton put a hand on each child's heads, closed his eyes and prayed to God to bless them. Then, after a moment's hesitation, he leaned over and kissed each boy on the forehead. "Sleep tight little men. Tomorrow, you go to school." Both boys were tired and fell asleep quickly.

9 OLD-FASHIONED SCHOOL

The next morning they were woken by Dr. Anton, who watched while Jacob put his prostheses on with some help from Mark. Jacob took his time and explained all the steps and why they were being done. After consulting with Dr. Anton, they decided to wear shorts, as it was quite warm and most of the boys their age wore shorts. Jacob figured that by now the other children were not only used to his prosthetics, but they also actually liked when he took advantage of them to play Tik-Tok more realistically. This was much the same as with children where he came from in the future, so he felt comfortable with this situation.

They washed up, brushed their teeth, and came to the table for breakfast. Dr. Anton was writing on a piece of paper with a quill pen. The boys were fascinated with this and showed Dr. Anton their ballpoint pens that they had in their packs. Jessica brought them toast made on a metal rack toaster over the stove and they had fried eggs with it.

As they ate, Mark watched Dr. Anton and looked around at everything in the room. "Jacob, everything is strange!" Mark stated.

"Yes, I know," Jacob answered. "It feels like we're in an old-fashioned movie."

There was a brief pause while Mark chewed, frowning and took another bite of egg. "If Daddy comes here and can't take us back, we'll have to stay here, won't we?" Mark asked.

Jacob looked worried. "I guess so, but at least we'll have Daddy here."

"Will Mommy come, too?" Mark asked.

Jacob bit his lip. His voice sounded exasperated as he answered. "I don't know, Mark. Maybe if Daddy knows he can't come back, Mommy will want to be with him and with us. But I'm sure he's trying to find a way to get us back. That's why we haven't seen him yet!"

Mark put his fork down and looked at Jacob with an anxious look on his face. "If we stay here, we won't ever have a Happy Meal, will we?" A tear was leaking down Mark's face.

Jacob stared at Mark. His first reaction was to laugh at the thought of missing a McDonalds Happy Meal. He hated to see Mark looking so miserable, so he managed not to laugh. Then suddenly it struck him what Mark was trying to say.

Dr. Anton was watching all this, and saw Jacob fight the urge to laugh, but then suddenly he went pale. "What's a 'happy meal'?" he asked. "Is that some kind of event, like a birthday?"

Jacob looked at him and shook his head. "It would be too hard to explain. It's something just for kids. But that's not really it." He looked as miserable as Mark, but at least he wasn't crying. "Everything we know is gone!"

Dr. Anton frowned and looked puzzled. "But you seem to recognize a lot of things and know what they are," the doctor protested.

Jacob shook his head. "We know them from old fashioned movies. But these aren't things we're used to living with. If we stay here, we'll never ride what we'd call a car, we won't fly on a plane, we won't eat at several restaurants that we like and most of the games and fun things we like won't be there. There won't be television." Jacob paused. "Do you have radio?"

Dr. Anton shook his head. "What's radio?"

Jacob thought hard. What did they call it in old fashioned movies? It came to him. "In one old fashioned movie they called it wireless."

Dr. Anton nodded. "We have wireless. It's used to send Morse code to ships."

"Do you send sound with it, like music and people talking about things?" Jacob asked.

Dr. Anton nodded. "Yes, it's been done. The same ship radios designed to receive morse code, a few years ago heard a man playing a violin."

Jacob nodded. "Yes, you can send sound. Voices, people talking, singing, music, all that can be sent wirelessly. And you can send pictures. When you send motion pictures over radio waves, it's called television, or TV for short. It's like that video I showed you on the iPhone."

Dr. Anton looked impressed, then suddenly pulled out his pocket watch. "It's time for you two to head to school or you might be late. We'll have to finish this conversation later." He looked at Mark. "Will you be OK little man? Do you want to stay here?" Dr. Anton asked, in a gentle voice.

"I'll be OK," Mark answered, immediately, wiping the tears off his cheek and taking one last bite to clear the egg off his plate. He was going to go with Jacob no matter what!

Dr. Anton gave them each a sandwich lunch and an apple and put them in a pail. Then he sent them out the door, explaining where to find the school. He needn't have worried however, because the children in the next house who had played with them the day before had been waiting for them and came running out to walk with them.

"Hey! Tik-Tok and Mark-Tok! Walk with us!" they shouted, running out.

The two boys forgot their troubles again, as they played with their new friends on the walk to school.

They arrived just in time for the bell to be rung. The teacher was Miss Prentice, the same one who taught Sunday school, so she already knew about Jacob's prosthetics. She welcomed them both and sat them with children their ages, to make it easier to teach them their materials.

Most of the children had seen Jacob at church, but there were a few who had only heard about him from the others. Some of them had refused to believe what they were told until they saw for themselves. Miss Prentice realized quickly that she'd have to get this over with, so she asked Jacob to explain what had happened to him and how his prosthetics worked.

Jacob was used to this, so he stood up and began to explain how he lost his arm and leg when he was a baby. One of the children questioned if he really wasn't just wearing a glove. Jacob laughed. "I can settle that for you!" He said. He grabbed his prosthetic arm with his left hand, and with a few twists, he pulled it off. He held his stump up. "Does it look like I have a hand?" he asked.

Half the children gasped. One little girl started to cry.

"You don't need to feel bad for me. I don't feel bad for me, and I'm okay with this. I didn't mean to upset you. I'll put it back on." Jacob put his arm back into the prosthesis, not wanting torment the little girl, twisting to get it in solidly. He was used to some people having trouble handling his missing limbs, and he was always sympathetic with them.

He held the prosthetic fingers up and flexed them. "I'm just making sure the sensors are connected right. The inside of this sleeve has sensors that detect when I flex little muscles in my stump, and they translate that into movement in the motors in my hand. That makes the fingers and thumb move."

Jacob went on to explain a bit of how his foot worked, including how it detected how he moved and helped him. Finally, he was done. "Does anyone have any questions?" he asked.

The little girl who had cried put her hand up. Jacob pointed at her.

"Did it hurt when you lost it?" she asked, looking worried.

"Yes, it did." Jacob answered, in a matter-of-fact way. "I was really little so I don't remember a lot, but I do remember crying because it hurt and wouldn't stop. The worst part was when my hand or foot would hurt or itch when it wasn't even there. Doctor Martin said it was called phantom pain. I still get that sometimes." Jacob grinned. "One of the funniest things is, when I feel an itch where there's no hand, it feels good when I scratch the prosthetic where it feels like the itch is! Our brain is really weird."

Another boy raised his hand. "Do you feel anything with your Tik-Tok hand or foot?"

Jacob shook his head. "Not with the foot, but I do with the hand. It has pressure sensors in the fingers and feeds signals into the nerves on my stump. It's pretty good but my real hand is the best."

Jack had his hand up, and Jacob pointed at him.

"You told me you had other artificial hands and feet. What are they like and when do you use them?" He asked.

Jacob nodded. "These two have some disadvantages. First, I have to charge the batteries, or they run down. It's a bit like Tik-Tok having to be wound up. They are both pretty heavy because of the motors and the batteries, so if they aren't working, they aren't so good. Also, a lot of times if I'm going to play hard, I have to take them off because these are pretty expensive, and I don't want to break them. And I can't put them in water because they have electronics. They can get rained on, but if I fall in a creek or pool or step in a deep puddle, I could wreck them. Also, I have a few prosthetics I use for special things like playing violin. I have one made to hold a violin bow. And I have a polymer blade leg with me at Dr. Anton's house. It's like a spring on the end of my stump that's the same length as my other leg. Sometimes I just take the hand off and play with my stump and one hand. If I go swimming, that's what I do. In fact, to swim, I skip all the prosthetics and just splash about with my stumps. I tried a prosthetic that was like a flipper, but I prefer to swim with no prosthetics. Just my bare foot and my bare stump."

Miss Prentice interrupted as a few more hands went up and said that they could ask more questions at recess. So, they started their lessons. The teacher only had one extra book, so she moved Mark next to Jacob and gave them a "McGuffey's First Eclectic Reader". They started reading the story in it and Mark gave Jacob a funny look. Jacob shook his head and put a finger to his lips.

Miss Prentice had heard both boys talking and realized that

they used English at a level that even many adults in the town did not. Jacob's little speech had settled that for her. Miss Prentice believed along with most of the town that the two boys were from a wealthy family, and it was only a matter of time before someone would find them, so she was anxious to make a good impression. Unfortunately, the spare reader was the first reader, so Miss Prentice had them go to a lesson near the end, on page 84, lesson LIX.

Jacob frowned. "Roman numerals! I haven't done those in ages." He whispered to Mark. "I think that's 59."

The story was about a girl called Mary and a little lame boy called Frank. Miss Prentice stood behind them and watched them read. Jacob would read to the end of the page, then grab it and wait. When Mark got to that page he'd say "Next" and Jacob would turn the page.

Miss Prentice watched them go through two pages then turn the page. She was amazed at how quickly Jacob got to the end and was ready to flip it, but equally amazing was the fact that Mark was only a few seconds behind him. Jacob was reading the book about three seconds per page with Mark a second or two behind him. They flipped the page, and she stopped them. "Wait. Mark, can you tell me what was on the previous page?"

Mark smiled at her and gave his version of the story, adding "She prob'ly blew the whistle too hard. My recorder sounds weird if you blow too hard."

Miss Prentice was impressed. She was also concerned that both boys were reading well beyond the reader. Her most advanced students were still in the fourth reader (there were five students at that level) and she had a feeling that Jacob at least would be ahead of it. She let them read on, but there was only one more story in that reader, so she told them to work back through the stories after that one.

Recess came and the children all spilled into the school yard. Jacob took a game he usually played with his friends called robot tag and changed it to Tik-Tok tag. You divided into two teams and had to walk like a robot and talk like a robot, and the person who was "it" could call "red team rewind" (it was supposed to be "recharge" for robot tag) and the red team would freeze while the blue team members had to find them and rewind them. Jacob told them they had to do three twists to rewind. This quickly became a tickle game, as the pretend rewinding would make some of the children squeal and giggle. Some of the children begged their friends to rewind them in their tummies.

A couple of older boys were standing to one side, feeling that their friends would think them too old for this game, but Mark saw them and ran over. "You gotta play! Please!"

With a laugh the older one, who had younger brothers and sisters said "Sure!" and in seconds all the older boys were happily playing, secretly enjoying the game an awful lot!

The bell rang and the children all groaned. That was a fun recess, and it went way too fast!

After recess Miss Prentice had them work on math. She quickly realized that Mark was doing math at the same level as some of her 12-year-olds, and Jacob was simply beyond anyone in the class. The oldest children in the class were 2 girls and a boy who were all 15. She was wondering what to do with him when he solved it for her.

One of the older children groaned that she couldn't get her problem. Jacob was next to the girl and started helping her. He quickly got her to understand the problem. He spent the day being the teacher's helper.

And so, the school day progressed.

...

Paul stepped in the door of Dr. Anton's office. The doctor was sitting at his desk looking at a very colourful book of some sort. Dr. Anton looked up, smiled, and put the book into a drawer before addressing the visitor.

"Hi Paul," he said standing up and shaking the inventor's hand, "what can I do for you?" He motioned him to a seat and sat down.

Paul sat down and came straight to the point. "I've been

hearing about a boy with some amazing prostheses, and being an inventor at heart, I was intrigued to know more. Mike the baker told me you paid them a visit over at the Rands. I was curious if you could share anything you knew about these prostheses. Maybe we could find a way to help war amputees if there's something useful there."

Dr. Anton thought for a second. He couldn't exactly reveal everything about this boy to the man, but Paul's idea was the same as his. The inventor might be helpful with his knowledge of engineering. His own doctor's skills weren't entirely up to the task.

Dr. Anton made up his mind. "Why don't you come by after supper and I'll let you look at the boy's prostheses. We can decide then what our next steps would be." He didn't think there'd be any risk in doing that.

Paul nodded. "I'll see you after supper, doctor." He stood up and let himself out of the study.

10 SHOW AND TELL

The children came home surrounded by two dozen of the town's children begging Dr. Anton to let them go play in the park until supper time.

Dr. Anton laughed and let them go. Jacob changed the batteries in his leg and arm before heading out.

When supper was almost ready, Dr. Anton headed to the park. He watched the children playing Tik-Tok tag and noticed that even the older children seemed to forget themselves and have fun with the game.

He felt bad having to interrupt them, but it was time to go home and eat.

He found himself laughing with the two boys and the two neighbour children walking with them, as they told excitedly about the games they played. Dr. Anton loved children, and to see the pure joy in their faces was a great pleasure for him.

Jacob and Mark and the neighbour children were disappointed when he told them that they would be busy after supper and wouldn't be able to come out to play.

The children enjoyed the supper, still excitedly relating all the fun they had had playing Tik-Tok. Finally, they were finished, and Dr. Anton sent them to the front room to play. He handed them a book.

"Here is a copy of Ozma of Oz. I believe you haven't read the whole thing?" Dr. Anton asked.

"No, we haven't." Jacob said with a big smile "We'll read it together."

As they were reading, they heard a knock at the door. The maid let a strange man in and took him to Dr. Anton's study. The boys didn't think anything of that, but a few minutes later both men came into the front room.

"Jacob and Mark, I'd like you to meet Mr. Rankin." Dr. Anton said. "He's an inventor, and I'd like him to see how your prostheses work."

The two boys put the book down. Jacob looked at Mr. Rankin. "Which one would you like to start with?" Jacob asked.

Mr. Rankin smiled. "Let's start with the leg."

Jacob explained the leg, using the same explanations he had used for Dr. Anton, but this man had a way of asking more questions and digging deeper. Jacob realized his mistake. The simplified version wasn't going to work for this man.

"I've been giving you the simple version," he said with a grin "and I just realized that you're looking for the more detailed version, and you seem to understand the detailed stuff, so let me start over."

"That would be great!" Mr. Rankin said.

Jacob thought for a second, then pointed at a part of the foot. "This is the battery compartment. It feeds into a…" he paused for a second "… Babbage engine just inside here."

"Wait," Mr. Rankin was frowning. "A Babbage engine is a huge affair, but that's in a very small foot. How can that be?"

Jacob sighed. "This is going to be difficult, knowing where to start. This is 'like' a Babbage engine, but it's really very different. It's completely electrical and miniaturized." Jacob thought for a second. "It uses silicon chips, in layers, with electrical circuits etched in, microscopically with chemicals. You use a 'program' to tell it what to do. That program is stored in memory chips. It's in a code that's designed for the computer chips – oh, we call the chips computers, because they compute. They're the Babbage engines."

Jacob paused and looked at Mr. Rankin. "Should I go on? I'm not really good at explaining the details of computers. I'm just a kid."

"Go on," Mr. Rankin said "you're doing very well. Tell me what the result of all that 'inference' is."

Jacob continued "The computer takes input from the muscles on my leg. It knows where I'm thinking of putting my weight, and how much. It analyzes that information and uses it to drive the electrical motors that push my foot. It does everything that a natural foot would normally do."

"What is the frame made of?" Mr. Rankin asked. "It looks lightweight, but it seems to be quite strong."

"It's made of an alloy of titanium and carbon steel," Jacob answered "which makes it very lightweight, but very strong. I can run and jump with it, and it works just like my real foot. Almost as good, and it never hurts!"

Mr. Rankin was lost in thought for a few minutes. "So, if I understand correctly, the key elements here are that thing you call the 'computer', the battery, as it must have a lot of power to drive the motors, the materials in that alloy, the sensors that sense what your leg muscles are doing, and the small but powerful motors?"

"Yes," Jacob answered, "that's right."

Mr. Rankin sat back and thought for several minutes. No one interrupted him. Jacob, Mark, and Dr. Anton watched him, quietly. Finally, he looked at the doctor. "Thank you for letting me see this, doctor," he said "I'm going to go away and think about this. I may have more questions in the next day or so." He pointed at Jacob's arm. "Is that more or less complicated than the leg?" he asked.

Jacob frowned, "I'm not really sure. I think it's about the same." He answered. "The part that sends feeling back to the nerves in my stump are definitely more complicated."

Mr. Rankin nodded. "I'm going to focus on just one. We'll look at the arm some other time. You are a very fortunate little boy to have those prostheses." He smiled at Jacob.

Jacob nodded. "I know, I'm really lucky. I don't take that for granted!"

"Can I see you walking with it?" Mr. Rankin asked.

"Sure." Jacob got up. "Where should I walk? Outside? Up the stairs?"

"Let's do the stairs first," Mr. Rankin said.

Jacob went to the stairs to the second floor and walked up them and down again.

"Can you do it a bit faster?" Mr. Rankin asked. "Only if it's safe, of course," he added.

Jacob smiled and ran up the stairs, and then ran back down. The sound of the motors was unmistakable, especially going up.

Mr. Rankin whistled. He hadn't expected the boy to actually run! "Other than the sound and seeing the metal on it, you can't tell he's got prosthetics! It's like he's got two normal legs!"

Dr. Anton nodded. "I didn't realize he could run the stairs like that! I'm not sure I'm excited about him doing that normally, but it was definitely interesting to watch."

"I don't need to see any more," Mr. Rankin said. "I'll go home and stew about this for a bit."

Dr. Anton saw Mr. Rankin out the door.

...

"OK," Andrew said, "We've got everything we need to open the time portal, but a bit higher elevation so we're at ground level this time. Keep it open while we're away. If anything happens, you guys need to reopen the portal. I've got the ATV, spare fuel, some gold bullion to trade for money, and provisions for a week, if I need it. And we'll test that the cellular repeaters work."

"Correct," Meg said, "and when he gets here, Tom will help you pull the ATV and other gear through."

"Where is he?" Rob asked.

"He said he needed to go back to the house and get something." Meg answered. "He said he'd be back in half an hour, so he should be here soon."

They all heard a door close upstairs.

"That must be him, now." Meg said.

A minute later, Tom Border came into the room. He was wearing camouflage gear and had an assault rifle with him.

"Tom! What on earth are you doing?" Andrew asked, shocked.

"I'm going with you," Tom said, calmly. "And I'm equipped to help ensure that if we encounter any resistance, we can overcome it! I've got another ATV ready to bring down the ramp, and spare fuel and provisions. Rob, please open the doors and I'll bring it in."

Andrew shook his head. "There's no way I'm allowing this, Tom, it's too dangerous! They're my boys and I'll get them back!"

Tom just smiled. "I have no kids of my own and I've got attached to yours. Besides, I've missed the excitement since retiring from my stint as a Navy Seal. I'm coming whether you like it or not."

He stood there, smiling.

Andrew sighed, knowing he was beaten. There was no way he was going to stop Tom, and truth be told, he was a little relieved. Tom had a cool head. "All right. I really appreciate this, Tom!"

Andrew turned to Meg, "Meg, how sure are you I'll wind up at the same place and time as before?"

"We won't know absolutely until we run it," she answered, "but there's no reason it would be significantly different. The big difference is that there's a bit of time drift if my calculations are correct. We can expect time there to have progressed either a bit slower or faster than here. I don't expect a lot of drift, but it could be up to half a day of drift, or more. We're anchored to the earth as our relative physical frame, so we should have the same place."

"Right." Andrew said. "We'll be here, but about one hundred years ago, give or take a decade. I have the old map, so I know the lay of the land. Let's get going, then."

...

Paul Rankin the inventor paused outside of Dr. Anton's house to stuff tobacco in his pipe and light it. He stood there, thinking hard. He grasped some of what he had seen and was amazed at it. He felt like his head was spinning! He had a good sense of what was practical with the tools, materials, and knowledge that he was aware of, and this clearly surpassed anything that he had seen. A Babbage engine that could do what this one was doing should have been the size of a large barn, not the size of a child's fingernail.

The other problem was that this was someone else's

invention. If they had any sense at all, their invention was patented, but it was just possible that they were using trade secret to protect their invention. The one downside of a patent was that it only protected you for a period of time, after which your invention became public domain.

Having worked for Mr. Bell, he was certain that he could become extremely wealthy if he was able to figure out and patent even one or two of the key parts that he had seen in that boy's prosthetic leg. He wasn't sure how to raise the question of patents without raising concerns.

As he stood there thinking, he noticed that Dr. Anton's window was open, and he could hear the two boys talking.

"Jacob," it was the little one talking, "do they have movies yet? They don't seem to have TVs."

"I think they have movies," the older boy was responding "but I don't think they had sound, and they sure didn't have colour."

There was a pause before the little boy spoke again. "I wish I was back in twenty twenty three where I belong. Why did Daddy have to send us here by accident?"

Jacob's voice sounded a bit annoyed. "There isn't a why. It's an accident! And he'll come for us and bring us home. He just has to figure out where we are. I've been thinking. When he sees that we're not in the waiting room, and that the furniture is gone, too, he'll know what happened. Then he'll have to prepare to get us back and come get us. I'm sure he'll do it soon."

Then Mr. Rankin heard Dr. Anton calling the two boys to get ready for bed. His pipe had gone out, and he put it in his pocket. That explained things. There was no way that the things he had seen could be done with technology as it currently existed. The patents would exist in the future, but that would not prevent him from using them now and getting very wealthy. He convinced himself that he could use them to benefit amputees, but he knew full well that his primary motivation was that he wanted to be a rich, famous inventor like Mr. Bell. He could think of many uses for the things he had seen that didn't involve prosthetics. He walked home, finally re-lighting his pipe when he arrived at his house, very pleased with himself.

11 SCHOOL AND A REQUEST

The next morning the boys left the house to find about half the school's children outside their house waiting for them. They played Tik-Tok all the way to the school.

Mark was helping a younger boy with his reading and Jacob was helping some of the older children with their reading and math for the morning.

Recess was another round of Tik-Tok tag, and this time the older children didn't have to be asked to join.

Jacob's leg gave off a warning tone just before recess ended, and he pretended to freeze. Jack figured out the solution and pretended to wind him up, tickling him the process, and getting a good giggle.

"Everyone, wind up!" Mark shouted, and they ended recess with a lot of shrieking and giggling as they all tried to wind each other up. Jacob changed the battery with everyone watching.

"My prostheses warn me when the battery is getting low, so I won't really run down like Tik-Tok, unless I ignore the beep and don't change my battery." He explained.

The day progressed well. There was a history lesson, and Jacob and Mark were at a disadvantage for once. It seems that they weren't well versed in events that felt important in 1910 but had been pretty well forgotten by the next millennium!

The Civil War was a big part of the history lesson, and they knew some of the details. Jacob realized that the Civil War to these children was a bit like World War II for Mark and him. It was fairly recent, and they had grandparents who had fought in it. It was fresher to these children than to the two of them. It also occurred to him that he shouldn't say anything about any World Wars to them. It wouldn't do to worry them about something they couldn't prevent. And so, their schooling continued.

...

Mike heard the bell on his shop door ring, and turned to see Paul Rankin coming in, smiling.

"Hi Mike," Paul said, "how'd you find yourself today?"

"Fine," Mike answered, "I just pulled back the covers and there I was!" he grinned at his own joke.

Paul laughed. "Good one! I'll have to remember that."

"Say," Paul said, "I've seen that boy, and had a session with him. I think there's some real potential in those limbs of his. The trick will be how to make them affordable. I think I'd have to convince someone in the government to fund some research."

Mike nodded, "So you've seen him walk? You can't tell he's got prosthetics until you see his prosthetics. If he wears gloves and long pants, he looks and moves perfectly normal."

"I noticed that" Paul said. "I had him go up and down the stairs in Dr. Anton's house. Then I asked if he could do it a bit quicker, and to the amazement of both Dr. Anton and I, he actually ran up and down the stairs! If you didn't know or see that his leg was prosthetic, or hear its motors, you wouldn't know he was an amputee! The motors were pretty noticeable when he was running. You can barely hear them when he just walks."

"So, do you think you can make something similar?" Mike asked.

"I don't know," Paul said "I'm not aware of electrical batteries that would hold enough power to drive that kind of energy. He's a little boy, but I think there's still a lot of force involved in what the foot is doing. The foot has electrical motors that are really small, yet drive a lot of power, and despite being small, it seems to be really robust. And he has an electrical inference engine he calls a 'computer' built in, that I'd have to analyze in more depth." He frowned. "I think I'd have to take it apart to figure it out, but I don't think the boy or Dr. Anton would go for that. If he only had a spare!"

Paul pointed at a loaf of bread, changing the subject. "Your bread smells so good, I'll have that loaf there, please."

"Sure," Mike replied. "I'll get that for you and wrap it in paper."

Paul paid and said goodbye as he left.

Outside, he noticed that the school children were playing in the field next to the school. He pulled out his pocket watch and noticed that it was just after noon. So, he walked over and stood under a tree to watch the children play.

You couldn't miss Jacob. He was wearing shorts, as were most of the boys. It was a very warm day for March, and around here, March could get quite warm. Jacob's metal leg was unmistakable, yet he ran and played much like the other children. His arm looked normal, too, except for the colour of the hand and fingers.

The more he thought about it, the more he became convinced that he had to examine the prosthetics more closely. The leg would be best, but that hand was pretty amazing, too. He had to have a couple of days with either of them.

Paul knew the value of a good invention. Even if he couldn't make a prosthetic out of it, there were enough innovations in here that he could make great value from any one of them. He had an engineering degree, and having worked for Mr. Bell, he knew how to do research, and had a good sense of the importance of the right materials and getting all the details right. His ticket to quick wealth was to figure out even one of the key pieces that made up the boy's prostheses and patenting it. Now that he knew that the prostheses were from the future, there would be no patents blocking him. He'd have an amazing edge on any other developers.

What if the boy and doctor wouldn't agree to let him examine the leg? How could he make sure he got access to it? He turned and walked to his house, puzzling out his options.

...

The school day ended, and Miss Prentice dismissed the children. She called Jacob and Mark and stopped them.

"I want to thank you for helping the other children with their work," she said. "You've been great helpers, and I think that having other children help them made it easier for some of them."

One of the children who had been helped heard this. "Yes, Jacob is so good at explaining!" she said.

A younger child chimed in. "Mark really helped me with my reading!" he said.

Jacob and Mark were a bit embarrassed with the attention, but also pleased with themselves.

They left the school and started walking back, playing Tik-Tok with a large group of children. Along the way, the two neighbor children mentioned that they had never read Ozma of Oz.

They arrived at Dr. Anton's house, and Jacob asked Dr. Anton if they could take the Ozma of Oz book out on the porch and read it with the neighbor children. Dr. Anton agreed, and the children all gathered on the porch, where Jacob began to read the story out loud with great animation.

They stopped at supper time, but as soon as they finished supper, they went back onto the porch and continued to read while it was light enough. It was quite warm for March, so the children weren't too cold on the porch as the sun went down.

As they were reading, Mr. Rankin, the inventor came by and knocked on the door. Dr. Anton let him in, and the two men went inside to the doctor's study to talk.

"I'll come right to the point, Anton," the inventor said. "I believe I can make headway with this, but I would need to take the prostheses and examine them more closely. I'd need to disassemble them."

Dr. Anton looked alarmed, and Paul saw this at once.

"I'm a professional engineer, Anton," he continued. "I've taken many things apart and reassembled them, and I'd be extremely careful. I'm mindful of the value of the prostheses and what they probably mean to the little lad, but this is too good of an opportunity to pass up. Just think of the good that could be done with this knowledge."

Dr. Anton shook his head. He was beginning to wish he had not humoured the inventor in the first place. "Paul, I can't let you do that without getting the boy's consent." he said. "After all, the prostheses are not mine, they are his. I can call him in, and you can have the conversation with him, but I'll support his right to say no."

Paul sighed. He had thought it would come to this. "Sure, let's ask him," he said.

Dr. Anton got up and went to the porch.

"Good grief! Children, you're reading in the dark! You'll go blind," he exclaimed, laughing. "Time to wrap this up. You can continue tomorrow. Jacob, Mr. Rankin would like to have another chat with us."

The children said their goodbyes, then the two boys came into the house. Jacob followed the two men into the study. Mark looked like he wanted to follow them, but Dr. Anton asked him to wait outside, and assured him they'd only be a few minutes.

In the study, he asked Jacob to sit down, and offered him one of the chairs.

When they were all seated, Dr. Anton spoke first. "Jacob, Mr. Rankin here is an inventor. He's an experienced engineer and is convinced that there are aspects of your prostheses that could benefit other people. He has a request that he wants to make of you. I'm going to assure you that I'll stand by your decision, regardless of what it is."

He turned to Mr. Rankin. "The floor is yours," he said.

Mr. Rankin smiled at Jacob. "My request, plain and simple, is to be able to have access to your prostheses to examine them more closely, uninterrupted. I would very carefully disassemble them, examine all the parts, and reassemble them, ensuring that they still worked when I was done."

Jacob was frowning through this. He turned to Dr. Anton. "You haven't told him the rather important secret about us, have you? I'd hope you hadn't."

Dr. Anton shook his head. "No," he answered slowly,

considering his words. He realized now that it was a mistake to involve Paul like this and wanted not to give anything important away.

Mr. Rankin almost said that he knew the secret but bit his tongue. He'd have to play along.

Jacob was trying to think how to word it, so he wouldn't give too much away. He looked at Dr. Anton. "So, when I say that it would take an army of experts, in many fields, one hundred years to create, let alone understand some of the technology behind my prosthetics, you'd understand why I'm saying that."

Dr. Anton sighed. "Yes, I think I understand. You don't need to defend your response, that's my job. Simply tell us your response."

Jacob looked at Mr. Rankin. He felt a little bit sorry for him, but there was no way that things would end well if he allowed it. "Sorry, Mr. Rankin, I can't let you do that. Firstly, this is a really expensive prosthetic, and to let someone who doesn't understand it take it apart would be irresponsible of me. And secondly, the complexity of some of the parts, and the miniaturization means that you would have no idea what you were looking at, and would probably damage some of the more fragile parts, without even knowing you were doing so, expert or not." He shook his head. "I have to say no, sorry."

Mr. Rankin sighed. It was what he had expected but wanted to try this first. He realized that the boy was probably right. The Babbage engine the boy called a 'computer' was something he would not be able to figure out, but even to figure out the battery, which he was certain he could do, and the materials, would make him very rich.

Mr. Rankin smiled at Dr. Anton. "Thank you for letting me make the request." He turned to Jacob. The boy's command of English surpassed many people he knew who had doctorates, and he had to admire him for that, and with the thought he gave a very respectful smile. "I understand what you're saying but believe I could have done the examination safely. If it's too complex and eludes me, so be it. Are you sure you won't reconsider?"

Jacob shook his head. "No, I have to stick to my decision. It's the right one."

Mr. Rankin nodded. "While I regret it, I respect your decision." He stood up and reached out a hand to Jacob. "You won't think ill of me for asking, will you?" he asked.

Jacob took his hand and shook it and smiled. "No, sir!" he answered. "I just wish I could give you a different response."

Dr. Anton saw Mr. Rankin out, then asked Jacob to come into the study. This time he let Mark join them. As soon as they were seated, Dr. Anton said. "Jacob, I want to apologize. When he came to me yesterday, I never thought it would come to this. I realized when he came to me today that I'd created a bit of a problem." He shook his head. "I guess I wanted to find a way to use what your prostheses could do to benefit some people I know, like Mike, and others like him."

Jacob sighed. "It is a bit of a weird thing," he admitted, "with me being from the future. I think you'll really have to wait a hundred years to see this stuff. I'm not sure what would happen if an invention we invented in the future, that was part of my prostheses, suddenly became past knowledge and wasn't invented by us. I don't know what would happen!"

Dr. Anton frowned as he thought about it. "I never thought of that," he said. "Changing the subject, a bit, would it really be that hard for him to understand your technology?"

Jacob nodded. It was tricky trying to explain it when he only understood it a little bit. "I've mentioned the chips. They have electrical circuits etched in chemically. I don't know if you can even see the etchings in the material. It might not be visible, even with a microscope, and it's so miniaturized that you would need a really good microscope. I don't think you actually have strong enough ones right now."

Dr. Anton nodded. "OK, so it would be too small and possibly invisible. That would be a problem."

Jacob nodded. "It gets worse. The circuits are not general purpose, you have to program them to do what you want."

"Like Babbage's inference engine?" Dr. Anton asked.

"Yes," Jacob responded, thinking hard, and talking slowly.

"Exactly, but it's not physically programmed, it's programmed electronically, with charges storing the memory." Jacob frowned. "I don't know exactly how it works, but there are billions of pieces of information stored, in a coded way, to tell the chips what to do. Some of those pieces of information are the program, and some are information we've provided it to work with. I don't think you'd understand the code, and you'd have to find where it's stored first. You'd probably erase it trying to read it, and then you'd never find it out. That's why it doesn't make sense to even try," he concluded.

"Right," Dr. Anton said. "I'll make sure that Mr. Rankin doesn't bother you again."

He let the boys play a little longer, then sent them to bed.

12 ANOTHER SCHOOL DAY

In the morning, the boys had their breakfast, and skipped out the door to meet their friends again. It had gotten even warmer. So much so that passing adults were commenting to each other about how unusual the warm spell was for so early in the year.

The children went to school playing Tik-Tok, and so started another fun day. Jacob and Mark both found that they were in demand for helping other children with learning some of the difficult skills, so they took on the role of teacher's helpers, again, and enjoyed it greatly.

At recess time, some of the children wanted to play a regular game of tag, so they played the game. The children were all amazed at how quickly Jacob could run with his artificial leg. The older boys could catch him, but some of the younger ones and even some of the slower older ones couldn't.

After recess, it was reading time. Miss Prentice had brought Jacob and Mark some books to read that would be more challenging, from the local library. She had brought two Jules Verne books, "Journey to the Centre of the Earth" and "Twenty Thousand Leagues Under the Sea". Mark took the first one, and Jacob took the second, and they began reading. Jacob was able to read his story easily, but Mark found it harder to follow his. He was still little, so he read a bit slower, and the story was written with a lot of grown-up words. Despite this, both boys soon got engrossed in the well-written stories and enjoyed the reading time.

So, their third day at the old fashioned school passed without incident.

...

"OK, turn it on," Andrew ordered. The soft hum of the time machine started, and instantly, they were looking into a forest. On the forest floor were the table and chairs from the waiting room.

Andrew reached down and picked up a cage with a bird in it. He had a long pole with a hook on the end. He used that to lift the cage and extend it into the time portal. The bird didn't seem to be harmed by passing through. That was good news. Test one had been passed.

The bird started singing, amongst the trees. As they pulled it back, they noticed that the tone changed pitch a bit lower as it came back across the field. Andrew looked at Meg, with a questioning look.

"Time drift," she said "like the Doppler effect. This confirms my suspicions. Different accelerations and directions in overall space are causing time to travel a bit faster there than here. You won't notice it when you're there. We may have to tune the radio frequencies for the cellular repeaters for the cell signals to go through. I suspect that the boys may have been there a bit longer than we've been preparing."

Next test, Andrew took a mirror on a selfie stick and pushed it into the portal. He was able to see himself and the room behind him. That was their second test passed. They were reasonably certain they could go both ways and expect to get back.

The next test was a big one. Andrew stepped across the time field, through the portal into the past. He then turned around and stepped back. No problems. Test three had passed.

"OK," he turned to Tom "let's get this furniture back." He frowned. "I thought there were magazines on the table."

"There were," Rob answered. "Someone must have taken them

with and left the furniture there. Might have been the boys."

The two men stepped in and started hauling the furniture back. Tom was looking around the area where the furniture had been. "It looks like a bunch of people have been trampling the ground here, and it looks like they came up from a trail below."

The next thing was to bring a large antenna through and set it up in the forest. While some of the others were setting it up, Andrew pulled out his phone. There was another directional repeater in their lab, so he would see if the signal would work. He was able to use the phone's data and dial his home, where he got an answering machine. He texted Meg, who texted back. Good. Now they just needed this repeater to give them better distance away from the portal.

Finally, they had the antenna up. This would allow them to get cellular signals for a couple miles around. Then several of them worked to get the ATVs to the trail. They drove them through the portal but had difficulty finding their way around some of the trees. A chainsaw helped, then they got a few shovels and started making a ramp. The bank down to the trail was too steep for the ATVs. It was going to be a lot of work to get down to the trail! They continued working on the ramp.

...

Dr. Anton was working in his study. It was Jessica's day off to visit her family, so with the children in school, he was on his own. It was a quiet day with no patients expected, and so he sat and read a medical journal.

He was engrossed in his reading but would likely not have noticed the front door opening quietly anyways. He did notice his study door open as Mr. Rankin stepped in.

He grabbed a bookmark and put it in his journal. "Hi Paul," he said, "what can I do for you? Have a seat."

Paul sat down. "I've been thinking about Jacob's prostheses and going through different ways that I can make at least a little headway with understanding them without dismantling them. And I'd like to continue in a less intrusive manner, if that's okay with you and him." He said.

Dr. Anton felt a bit of relief. He was still concerned about how this would play out. If Paul was okay with understanding it from the outside, then that would be fine.

"Paul pulled out his pocket watch." I guess school just got out and they'll be here in a bit. He looked out the window. "Yes, I can see in the distance, they're all leaving now. So, I hate to do this, but I see no other way to get hold of this amazing technology." He pulled out a gun from his pocket.

Dr. Anton looked stunned. "What are you going to do?" he asked, shocked.

"I'm not going to harm you, if you do as you're told." Paul said, "I'm going to tie you up and gag you. I'll do the same with the boys and take the prostheses. I understand the boy has one that's not electronic, so he'll still be able to move around. By the time anyone finds and unties you, or you get out of my bindings, I'll be long gone."

Dr. Anton was livid, but there was nothing he could do. Paul was quick and efficient. He had spent some time in the military and knew how to tie someone up very efficiently.

...

School had ended, and the boys headed to Dr. Anton's home, with their school friends playing Tik-Tok with them.

As the boys were approaching their home, a loud PING sound was heard in Jacob's pocket. He and Mark froze and stared at each other. A text message???!! Here???!!! Jacob pulled it out and squealed "Daddy! Mark! He's texted us, he's coming for us!"

The message read:

Have come to find you. Found the couch and chairs. If you see this, text where you are.

Jacob texted back:

Staying with doctor in town. Down trail from you is

farmhouse. They'll tell you how to find us. They were good to us.

"Can I see?" Mark asked, excitedly.

Jacob handed the iPhone to Mark so he could see the messages himself. The phone had barely one bar, but that was enough for the texts to go through.

The children around them asked what was happening, and Jacob tried to explain that their father was sending them wireless messages that he was nearby and coming for them.

"You mean like a telegraph?" one of the children asked.

"Yes," Jacob smiled. It was a good comparison. "Exactly like that!"

"Does that mean you'll be leaving us?" one of them asked, sadly.

Jacob looked sad. "Yes, it does. But I really want my family. You understand that don't you?"

The children all agreed.

13 DANGER AND RESCUE

Andrew turned the corner and saw the farmhouse, just as his son's text message had said. There were three children playing outside, but they stopped what they were doing to stare at the two ATVs. The older boy ran over.

"Are you looking for Jacob and Mark?" the boy asked. "Are you their daddy, Mr. Harper?"

"Yes, they told me they are at the doctor's house in town. Can you tell me where that is?" Andrew asked.

The boy turned to a man and woman who had come out on the porch. "Mommy, Daddy, can I go with Mr. Harper and show them where the doctor's house is?"

"You may," The man answered, then looked at Andrew. "Your boys are fine young men, but they really belong in their own time and place. I'm glad you came for them. We were all worried for them."

"Thank you," Andrew said, then turned to Jack. "What's your name son? Come on up here and sit on this seat."

"I'm Jack Rand" Jack answered. Andrew buckled the boy in, and they started off.

Jack had never travelled so fast in his life. He'd run a horse at a gallop, but this was way faster, and smoother! He was having the time of his life and told them where to turn. They'd be in town in just a few minutes!

...

Mr. Rankin was getting impatient. His train would be along shortly, and these children were shrieking and playing at something. He needed them to come home so he could take the prostheses and get away. Finally, the children resumed walking. Some of them looked sad about something. They all gave hugs and handshakes, and parted ways outside the house, and the two boys ran in. Paul went back into Dr. Anton's study.

"Doctor! Doctor!" Jacob called, running in, then paused, shocked to see Dr. Anton tied up on the floor and Mr. Rankin standing there, holding a gun. Mark ran in behind him.

Mr. Rankin stepped behind them and shut the door. He waved a hand at the two chairs. "Have a seat, children." He said.

Mark was starting to cry, frightened.

Jacob was furious. "You tied up Dr. Anton! How could you! And you're scaring my little brother!"

Mr. Rankin calmly replied. "I insist you sit down."

"I'm not doing anything you say!" Jacob fumed.

Mr. Rankin took Mark by the shoulder and pointed the gun at his tummy. "Maybe this will make you reconsider." He said.

Mark's eyes grew big and round as the tears continued to run down his cheeks. He turned pale and a frightened gasp was all the sound he made as he turned his frightened eyes to Jacob.

Jacob burst into tears and sat on the chair. "Don't hurt my little brother! Please!" he begged. His anger was mixed with horror at the thought that this man might hurt Mark. "I'll do what you say, just please don't point the gun at him."

"That's more like it," Mr. Rankin said, pointing the gun away. "You can sit here." He put Mark in the other seat, then turned to face Jacob.

He pointed the gun right at Jacob's tummy from several feet away, and Jacob began to feel terribly uncomfortable with the gun pointed at him like that. The tears continued oozing down his face.

"I'll start by admitting that I overheard the two of you talking the other night, after I had visited you the first time, and I realize that you are from the future. I also realize that there's no way I can fully reverse engineer your prostheses. On the other hand, there are aspects of your prostheses that I'm sure I can figure out, and I could patent, and make great money from, and I intend to do so. If I can use them to that end, I'll make a point of helping amputees. I think I should be able to achieve some success at that. I also realize that you may be returning soon, and my opportunity to benefit mankind may disappear."

An angry noise came from Dr. Anton, through his gag.

Mr. Rankin looked at Dr. Anton. "Yes, I know the great secret that I was not supposed to know. I had no doubts about it either. I understand the sheer impracticality of trying to make what they have with today's tools and materials. But I know that I can make great gain with this. Even if I have to do it from another jurisdiction."

Mark was still holding the iPhone that Jacob had passed to him and had slid it to silent mode. Mr. Rankin wasn't looking at him, so he carefully texted, looking down as little as possible:

Daddy man holding us up wth gun in doctors hose and wants to steel Jacs pros. Hurry

He wasn't good with spelling big words and his hands were shaking. Autocorrect fixed a few words and messed up "house". He sent the message and only looked down twice. Then he hit the home button so the message would clear, in case the man looked at the iPhone.

Mr. Rankin finished his speech and turned to Mark. "I'm afraid I'm going to have to tie you up young man." He turned to Jacob who was protesting and said, "I won't hurt him, but I need to restrain him."

Mark managed to lock the iPhone before the man took it from him.

Mr. Rankin tied and gagged Mark quickly, putting the iPhone in his pocket. "I'll examine this later." He said. Then he turned to

Jacob. "Please take your arm and leg off and hand them to me." The man pointed the gun at Jacob's tummy again.

Jacob did as he was told, sobbing with anger and fright. Mr. Rankin put them in a large duffel bag he had brought with him. Then stepped over to Jacob.

"I'm going to tie you up now. I won't hurt you, but I'll have to tie you up a bit differently, I just realized." He frowned. "I can't tie your arms together," he murmured. "You only have one. Same problem with your legs." He wound up tying Jacob's left arm and leg to the chair he was in, then gagged him. He was aware that it might not hold very long, but he was worried he'd miss the train. His training assumed the person you were tying had two arms and two legs. Then he took the duffel bag, stuffed the gun in his pocket and headed to the back door of the house. The train station was across the street and the train would be there in just a few minutes. He just had time to make the station.

As he stepped out of the house, something heavy hit him on the back of the head. He went down, with his head spinning. He'd dropped the duffel bag. He found himself pinned down and was conscious of the gun and iPhone being pulled out of his coat pocket. He heard the voice of Mike the baker yelling for help. His head began to clear.

He heard several people running up.

"Open the duffel bag." Mike's voice said from his back.

"What on earth is this?" a voice asked.

"Those are the prostheses from that little amputee boy who's been staying with the doctor." Mike responded. "I was coming over to Dr. Anton's place to talk to him, when I hear this man threatening the children. I clobbered him with this two by four when he stepped out with the stolen limbs. Someone go free Dr. Anton and the boys. I believe he tied them up if I heard what he was doing correctly. And someone, please get the sheriff."

One of the men who had run up, went into the house. He found the study quickly, and in a minute had freed all three of them.

Jacob hopped out on his one leg, tears still streaking his face, followed by Mark and Dr. Anton. The adults around him were impressed at how easily Jacob moved with just one leg and one arm, and very angry at Mr. Rankin. Jacob started putting his prostheses back on.

Mr. Rankin stayed pinned down, unable to move for several minutes. Then he saw the sheriff running up.

The situation was explained to the sheriff, and he pulled out his handcuffs and put them on Mr. Rankin.

Meanwhile Jacob took his iPhone and checked the messages and saw what Mark had sent.

"Brilliant job, Mark!" he said.

Mark looked pleased at the praise.

Jacob sent another message:

We were rescued. Please come quickly.

Jacob put his iPhone in his pocket. The train was pulling into the station, so they didn't hear the ATVs pulling up until they were almost there.

"Jacob, Mark, are you two OK?" It was Jack calling them.

"Daddy! Daddy!" The two boys shrieked when they saw their dad.

The sheriff meanwhile was white with rage as he pulled Mr. Rankin to his feet. "So, Mr. Rankin, you saw fit to attack the town's good doctor, and try to rob a little crippled boy!" the sheriff said, looking grim. "This will not sit well with the magistrate! Do you have anything to say for yourself."

Mr. Rankin was frantically thinking what he could say. This was not going to end well, but he had one more card to play. "Sheriff, what you don't realize is that these boys here are from the far future."

The sheriff looked at Dr. Anton, who shook his head sadly. He needed to play down what Mr. Rankin was saying. "He's delusional." he said, shaking his head sadly.

Mr. Rankin continued "There is no way that what they have could have come from this day and age. The boy's prostheses are simply too advanced! You have to believe me!"

The sheriff laughed, grimly. "Mr. Rankin. That would not excuse your conduct. Anyways, I've been to an exposition in Chicago where I've seen some of the amazing things that electricity can do. You're simply out of touch with today's world." He turned to Dr. Anton. "Is he right in his head?"

Dr. Anton shook his head. "No," he replied. "I'd say he's delusional, and dangerous. No need to hold these good people here. You've seen for yourself what he's done, and I can vouch for him tying me up at gunpoint. I believe these children want to go home to their families. They've experienced enough distress."

"Right-o!" the sheriff said, and turning to Jacob, Mark, Rob, and their dad, he said "Off you go! We'll take it from here!" He shook his head. "Those are quite the motor cars you've got there!" he added.

Andrew thanked the sheriff. He also thanked Dr. Anton for taking good care of his boys, then they loaded Jack and Mark on Andrew's ATV, and Jacob on Tom's and they rode off, going slowly, so the constable would think they were ordinary motorcars.

Once they got out of town, they sped up.

Jack turned to Jacob. "I can't believe how fast these things go! Are these future motorcars?" he asked.

Jacob laughed "No, these are called all-terrain-vehicles, or ATVs for short. Real cars can go a lot faster, but kinda need a real road, or good gravel, at least. These can get around on pretty rough ground."

They stopped at the farmhouse to drop Jack off. There Jacob and Mark gave the Rand family all a big hug, and a tearful goodbye.

Andrew and Rob shook Mr. Rand's hand.

"I really appreciate you taking care of my boys," Andrew said. "I'm really obliged to you!"

Mr. Rand laughed. "Your boys are a delight, and so very polite. They were really a pleasure to care for. We only had them for one night, but we got quite attached to them!"

"Yes, but you believed their story, and took care of them," Andrew said. "That made the difference for them!"

Mark gave Timmy a big hug, snuck his toy car into the toddler's pocket, and whispered to him. "This is for you, to remember us, and to play with!" He gave the grinning child a big grin.

Then they were off. The Rand family asked to follow them and watch them return, so they drove slowly as the family walked with them, the Rand children getting a ride on the ATVs. They drove the ATVs up the ramp. There, where the furniture had been, was a large pole with a big dish on it, and a funny space, like a hole, in the middle of the air, and the inside of a building could be seen through it, with several people in it.

One more set of goodbyes and hugs.

"Good-bye," Jacob said in his best Tik-Tok, stilted voice. "We will ne-ver for-get you!"

This got giggles from the Rand children and laughs from all the adults.

"Good-bye Jacob Tik-Tok, and Mark-Tok," Jack responded, giggling though his tears. "We'll never forget you, either!"

The time travelers rode the ATVs through the time portal into the lab. Tom and Rob came back and pulled down the transmission tower, and they pulled it back through the portal. Then, with a last wave and "good-bye" to the Rand family, they closed the portal.

...

Mike stumped into Dr. Anton's study, closed the door behind himself and sat down.

"I spoke with Paul in prison." He said "I cannot defend what he did, but he made a strong case for his claims that the boy's prostheses were not practical with today's technology. I'm not here to defend him or take his position, but I'd like to know if someone out there has prostheses that do what Jacob's prostheses could do. Is there any hope I could get something like that in my lifetime?"

Mike waited for Dr. Anton to answer.

Dr. Anton frowned. He looked at Mike and made up his mind.

"What I'm going to tell you here, I'll say just for you. I will deny saying it to anyone else, but because I understand what your interest is, and trust you to be circumspect, I'll put it to rest for you."

Dr. Anton stood up and walked to the corner of his study. "Hang tight while I get something from my safe," he said.

Dr. Anton turned the combination. The safe was positioned so that no one sitting in a guest seat in the study could see what number he was turning. He pulled out a couple of magazines and children's books and brought them to the table. He passed them to Mike.

"Take a look at the pictures in that." Dr. Anton said, "When you've done that, look at the date on the magazines and the copyright dates on the children's books."

Mike whistled as he looked at the pictures. He did as he was told, then passed them back to Dr. Anton. "So, I won't see anything like this in my time!" he said, looking sad.

"No," Dr. Anton answered. "And I'm sorry. I let Paul look at the prostheses because I wanted people like you to have the benefit of the technology. I realize now I should never have trusted him. Those prostheses will be state-of-the-art in just over one hundred years, in twenty twenty three.

Mike stood up. "Thank you for clearing that up for me, doctor. Paul won't get any support from me. That was a cruel, evil thing he tried to do, and this doesn't excuse it."

14 FULL CIRCLE

It was a week later, and their mother had returned from her conference in Europe. Jacob and Mark had just returned home from school. As they got out of the car, a family stepped out of a minivan parked in front of their house and walked up to them. There was a couple who got out with a boy about Mark's age and a girl about Jacob's age, and an older woman with a cane. The little boy was carrying a box.

"Are you Jacob and Mark Harper?" The elderly woman asked the two boys.

"They are," their mother replied. "What do you want with them?"

The family was smiling, but with a look like they were seeing a celebrity.

"We would like to return something that you two left behind just over a hundred years ago," The older woman said. She pointed at the box the little boy was carrying. "My grandson has the things in a box here."

Jacob stared at the boy. "Who gave you what was in the box?"

"Well," the little boy replied, "my great grandfather got the books and magazines from Dr. Anton, and got the car from great uncle Timmy when he got older, and he insisted that when we got to this date, one week after you left, we should give the things back."

Jacob's mom shook her head. "I don't believe this! I know what happened, but it still blows my mind. You might as well come in. What are your names?"

The elderly lady responded. "I'm Martha Rand. My father was

Jack Rand. This is my daughter Elizabeth Bond, son-in-law Tom Bond, and my granddaughter and grandson Emily and Timothy Bond. Timothy is named after his great-grandfather, who was my father, and a friend to you two boys."

As they walked in, Martha continued. "My father would tell us stories about you two little boys and how you played Tik-Tok, and I told my children and my grandchildren here the same stories. We were always looking forward to the day we got to meet you and return the stuff."

"Sometimes we thought we'd bust, waiting!" Emily said, laughing.

Inside the house, Timothy handed the box to Jacob. "You can open this. There's something specially for Mark in there, though." He said.

Inside the box were the magazines and children's books from the waiting room. They had an old, faded look, and appeared to have been worn a bit from use, but they were in okay shape.

Martha continued. "We got quite wealthy. We'd see a company listed in the magazine and invest in it, knowing that it would do well in the long run."

As Jacob pulled the last magazine out, Mark was looking in the box and he squealed with delight. There, at the bottom, was his toy car. It too, looked old and played with, yet it was his same old car, that he had given to Timmy, just a week ago.

"Oh, wow!" Mark exclaimed. "I just realized that although I gave this to Timothy just a week ago, it's been over a hundred years for the toy!"

And there was a letter in the box, that read as follows:

Dear Jacob Tik-Tok and Mark-Tok,

I'm now over 60 years old, and Dr. Anton long ago gave me the magazines and children's books that you left behind. We felt it best to keep them out of the wrong hands. I'm arranging with my family that these will be sent to you a week after the date that you got lost. Timmy and Alice

both say hi. For a long time we played Tik-Tok, and we've always enjoyed our little family secret.

I'm also including some pictures and stories about what happened to us, and hope that my family will share some of their family stories with you, too.

As a grown-up now, I can only imagine how awful your father must have felt, but his loss was definitely our gain. You gave us memories that have lasted our lifetime, and made for great stories for our children. Our children will be older than your father, but if they are still alive they, and their children, would love to meet you.

Hope you have a long, joyful, prosperous life, my little Tik-Toks.

Love,

Jack, Tim and Alice.

ABOUT THE AUTHOR

Raised in the 1960s in the Lower Mainland of British Columbia, Robert Houben developed a passion for reading, storytelling, and performing music since his childhood. From being a teenage leader-in-training for scouting to becoming a scouter and youth group leader in different churches, as well as fulfilling roles as a parent and uncle, he has always cherished the art of crafting and sharing stories for children.

His continued work with children and youth has enabled him to view different experiences from a child's viewpoint and express them in a way that is engaging and fun for children.

Now, Robert is excited to extend this love of storytelling to a wider audience.

Robert can be reached through his website at **www.roberthouben.com**, and his Twitter account @houbenator or at his Amazon Author Page:

https://amazon.com/author/roberthouben

ACKNOWLEDGMENTS

I would like to acknowledge the many people over the years who set an example for me of ad-hoc story telling. This includes my father, and scouters and other volunteers, too numerous to name in detail, who told stories during campfires, and by example, taught me their craft.

I would also like to acknowledge all the authors whose books I read over the years, including those whose stories I read to my children when they were young (we read many an Edith Blyton story together.)

I would also like to acknowledge family members, including my wife, my son and my sister and brother-in-law, who proof-read and provided editing advice for several of my stories.

Lastly, I wish to acknowledge the many beavers, cubs, scouts, and venturers who have enjoyed my stories over the years. Their enthusiasm and joy have been an inspiration to me.

www.ingramcontent.com/pod-product-compliance
Lightning Source LLC
LaVergne TN
LVHW091034150826
845672LV00006BA/1812

* 9 7 8 1 7 7 5 1 5 7 5 6 4 *